D0578089

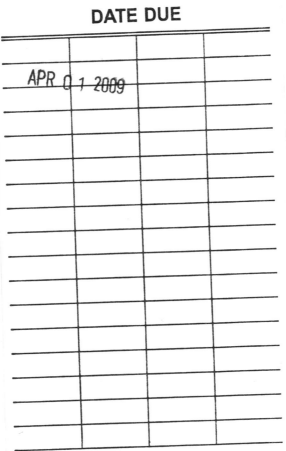

DATE DUE

APR 0 1 2009			

Demco, Inc. 38-293

OUR FRAGILE PLANET

ENDANGERED HABITATS

Jenny Tesar

Series Editor:
Bernard S. Cayne

A Blackbirch Graphics Book

Facts On File®

AN INFOBASE HOLDINGS COMPANY

Copyright © 1992 by Blackbirch Graphics, Inc.
Text copyright © 1992 by Jenny Tesar

All rights reserved. No part of this book may be reproduced or utilized in any
form or by any means, electronic or mechanical, including photocopying,
recording, or by any information storage or retrieval systems, without permission
in writing from the publisher. For information contact:

Facts On File, Inc.
460 Park Avenue South
New York, NY 10016

Library of Congress Cataloging-in-Publication Data
Tesar, Jenny E.
    Endangered Habitats.
    (Our fragile planet; 4/by Jenny Elizabeth Tesar; series editor, Bernard S.
Cayne.)
    Includes bibliographical references and index.
    Summary: Examines the various types of Earth's habitats, the complex
relationships of plants and animals found in them, and how man's activities
can upset or destroy fragile ecological balances.
    ISBN 0-8160-2493-6
    1. Habitat (Ecology)—Juvenile literature. [1. Habitat (Ecology). 2.
Ecology. 3. Man—Influence on nature.] I. Title. II. Series: Tesar, Jenny E.
Our fragile planet; 4.
QH541.14.T47   1991   90-47189
333.95—dc20

A British CIP catalogue record for this book is available from the British Library.

Facts On File books are available at special discounts when purchased in bulk quantities
for businesses, associations, institutions, or sales promotions. Please contact our Special
Sales Department in New York at 212/683-2244 or 800/322-8755.

Design: Blackbirch Graphics, Inc.

Printed in the United States of America

RRD PKG 10 9 8 7 6 5 4 3 2

This book is printed on acid-free paper.

CONTENTS

1

WILL THERE BE A TOMORROW?

"Upon entering their habitat one sees individuals on all sides. They seem to appear from nowhere, perch a few moments on the tops of the vegetation, and scold continuously. Here and there males chase the females in zigzag courses, flying low and very swiftly just above the grass tops, sometimes for several hundred yards or more. Others from many directions simultaneously sing their rasping, far-carrying songs from prominent perches atop grass or rush stems."

Bird-watcher Donald J. Nicholson wrote these words in the 1930s as he described small, enchanting birds known as dusky seaside sparrows. The sparrows were plentiful then. Thousands lived in coastal marshes near Titusville, Florida.

Today, only pictures and the words of people like Nicholson are left. There are no dusky seaside sparrows. The birds are extinct. The last dusky seaside sparrow died in 1987.

The species was the victim of human activities. Some of the salt marshes in which the sparrows lived were impounded and flooded in an effort to control mosquitoes at the Kennedy Space Center. A highway, built to connect the space center and Disney World, destroyed more marshes. Real estate developers drained some of the marshes. A fire started by a rancher to eliminate brush spread into part of the sparrows' nesting areas, burning almost 2,000 acres (809 hectares).

Opposite page:
The actions of humans create the greatest threat to the world's natural habitats. If left unchecked, these actions could eventually result in a planet that is barely inhabitable by life.

5

Failure by government officials to clear fire lanes led to further destruction when more fires occurred.

With fewer nesting areas and diminishing food supplies, the number of dusky seaside sparrows quickly declined. It took less than 50 years for a thriving species to be wiped off the face of the Earth.

For dusky seaside sparrows, there is no tomorrow. The species no longer exists. A similar fate faces thousands of other plant and animal species whose survival is also threatened by the activities of people. They face the possibility that they too will soon be extinct.

These species range from the small and drab to the large and beautiful, from the unknown to the famous. Among these threatened creatures are all five living species of rhinoceroses. Various species of rhinos have lived on Earth for more than 50 million years. At the beginning of the 20th century, millions of rhinos roamed through parts of Africa and Asia. As the 20th century nears its close, however, fewer than 11,000 of the animals remain. And the numbers continue to decline.

Most threatened of the rhinos is the Sumatran rhino, or hairy rhino. Unlike other rhinos, the Sumatran rhino is covered with a coat of hair. It is related to the extinct woolly rhino that roamed across Europe during the ice ages. As the 1990s began, the Sumatran rhino was the rarest large mammal in the world. Fewer than 60 of the animals remained.

Rhinos are being crowded out of their natural habitats as exploding human populations clear land for farms and other needs. They are also being slaughtered for their horns—a rhino horn can be sold for thousands of dollars in the Far East, where people believe that the powdered horn has magical powers, and in Yemen, where a dagger handle made from rhino horn is a status symbol.

Will these creatures have a tomorrow? Will they survive? Conservation experts who gathered in 1991 to discuss ways to save the rhinos said that the situation is not hopeless. Strong protection measures may enable the five species to recover. At the beginning of the 20th century, the Indian rhino was almost extinct. Thanks to protective measures such as the creation of refuges, the population of Indian rhinos has grown to about 2,000. Though an encouraging improvement, this is still a very small population; the species is still endangered. Each year, poachers kill some of the animals and development shrinks their habitat. The rhinos are also threatened by political unrest, disease epidemics and natural disasters.

Scientists estimate that tens of thousands of species of plants and animals are in danger of becoming extinct in the near future. These organisms are in peril because of humans; if they are saved, it will also be because of humans.

Will There Be Room for Rhinos?

Living things are found everywhere on Earth. A black rhinoceros charges through brush country in Kenya. A hairbrush cactus blooms on a desert in Mexico. A howler monkey lets out a roar from the top of a tree in a Panamanian forest. Fish with built-in lights hunt for food in the deep, black waters of the Pacific Ocean. A thicket of raspberry plants on a Scottish hillside yield masses of juicy fruit. A swarm of springtails forms a golden carpet on the snow high on a mountain in Canada.

UNDERSTANDING RELATIONSHIPS

To understand how the activities of humans affect other organisms, it is necessary to understand how living things relate to one another and to their environment. The study of these relationships is called ecology. The term is believed to have been suggested by the German biologist Ernst Haeckel in 1869. It comes from two Greek words: *oikos*, which means "house" or "place to live," and *logos*, which means "science" or "study."

There are numerous branches of ecology. For instance, freshwater ecology deals with interrelationships among organisms that live in lakes and rivers. Grassland ecology studies organisms that live in prairies and steppes. Population ecology focuses on changes in the numbers of individuals of a species and the reasons for such changes. Community ecology studies the ways in which organisms within a community interact with one another. Medical ecology studies the ecology of mosquitoes, ticks and other animals that carry diseases that infect people.

Scientists who specialize in ecological studies are called ecologists. Many other scientists also do research and gather information important to ecologists. Marine biologists study life in the sea. Ornithologists study birds. Ethologists study animal behavior. Bryologists study mosses. Climatologists study various climates, how they change and the causes for these changes.

Transplant the black rhino to a Canadian mountain, however, and it would soon die. Put the cactus into the Pacific, and it too would die. Each organism has a particular home, or habitat, to which it is best adapted. Move that organism to another habitat, and it may be unable to survive.

The organism may also be unable to survive if its natural habitat is changed. Howler monkeys cannot survive when the rain forests in which they live are cut down. Deep-sea fish cannot survive if poisoned by radiation leaking from a nuclear

THE PRAIRIE HABITAT

The prairie is an example of a specific habitat and ecosystem. Each organism depends on and contributes to the balance of the prairie.

waste dump. If organisms are to survive, their habitats must also survive.

There are numerous threats to habitats. Some are natural threats, such as devastating storms. But the greatest threats are created by people. People harm habitats in many ways. Housing developments cover grasslands. Dams flood canyons. Strip mines destroy hillsides. Ski resorts cut swaths in forests. Oil spills pollute beaches.

In some cases, the habitats are completely destroyed. The many plants and animals that lived there are left homeless. In other cases, habitats are reduced in size. This in turn reduces the number of plants and animals that can live in the area.

The harm caused by human activities often affects habitats far from the location where those activities are taking place. Pollution from Soviet factories kills trees hundreds of miles away in Finland. Demand for teak furniture in North America destroys Asian forests. Soil eroded from deforested areas in the Amazon River basin smothers Caribbean coral reefs. As these habitats are damaged, all the organisms that live within them are affected. Some may survive and even thrive as the habitats change. Most, however, are harmed.

Natural habitats have been harmed or destroyed with increasing speed as human populations have expanded. In 1830, there were about 1 billion people on the Earth. By 1930, the number had doubled to 2 billion. By 1990, the human population had jumped to 5.3 billion.

By the year 2000 there will be 6.25 billion people. These people will need homes, food, water, energy for heat and light, clothing, medical supplies and facilities, roads, schools—the list of basic necessities is lengthy. In addition, people want television sets, toys, private cars, jewelry, microwave ovens, throw-away plastic cups, golf clubs, picnic coolers, comic books and many other nonessential items. Where will the natural resources required to meet the needs and demands of future generations come from? Where will the garbage and other wastes of future generations be put? Which habitats and which organisms will disappear to meet the needs and demands of people?

Will there be room for rhinos and other wild creatures?

"Grandfather, Great Spirit, fill us with light. Teach us to walk the soft earth as relatives to all that lives."
    –Dakota Indian prayer

2

THE NECESSITIES OF LIFE

Scientists have named and described about 1.4 million species of living things. Many additional species remain to be discovered and identified. Estimates of the total number of species on Earth range from about 5 million to 80 million.

Earth's organisms include ducks and daffodils, monkeys and monkeypod trees, rice and raccoons, seals and seaweed. These organisms range from bacteria so tiny that they can only be viewed through high-powered microscopes to the 120-ton blue whale, the largest animal that has ever lived on Earth.

Despite great differences in size, shape and structure, all living things share certain traits. First, with the exception of viruses, all living things are made up of cells. Some, such as bacteria and yeast, are composed of a single cell. Others, from lions to dandelions, are composed of many different kinds of cells. The cells contain organized structures and various chemicals. For example, all living things contain nucleic acids. These complex molecules include deoxyribonucleic acid (DNA) and ribonucleic acid (RNA). DNA and RNA store genetic information, control cellular activity and direct the making of proteins.

A second trait shared by living things is the ability to grow and develop. An oak tree begins life as an acorn. If conditions

Opposite page:
In most optimal habitats, plants and animals coexist in a complex network of interdependence and cooperation. Here, hippos share a watering hole with various species of birds in Africa.

11

are right, that acorn will develop into a tall tree with numerous roots, branches and leaves. When a red kangaroo is born, it weighs 0.03 ounce (1 gram) and is less than 0.8 inch (2 centimeters) long. When it is fully grown, it may weigh 200 pounds (91 kilograms) and be 80 inches (210 centimeters) long.

A third trait is the ability to respond to stimuli in their environment. A geranium turns its green leaves toward light. An amoeba moves toward food. A herd of antelopes runs away from a lion.

A fourth trait is the ability to reproduce more creatures of their own kind. Reproduction ensures that the species will continue to survive. Some species produce huge numbers of eggs. A female blue crab mates only once in her life, but she produces a mass of about one million eggs. Of these eggs, however, perhaps five will eventually develop into mature crabs. The rest will be eaten or will die because of unfavorable environmental conditions.

Finally, all living things have the ability to obtain and use energy, through a process called metabolism. The ultimate source of energy is the sun. This energy is trapped in food. When the food is broken down in cells, energy is released.

Meeting the Need for Food

Organisms can be divided into three groups, based on their source of food: producers, consumers and decomposers.

Producers

Producers are organisms that make their own food. Green plants and algae are producers. They make food through a process called photosynthesis—a name derived from two Greek words meaning "putting together with light." There are four basic requirements for photosynthesis: (1) a source of energy, which is usually sunlight; (2) water; (3) carbon dioxide; and (4) a green pigment called chlorophyll.

During photosynthesis, light energy absorbed by the chlorophyll is used to break apart water molecules into hydrogen and oxygen. The oxygen is given off as waste. The hydrogen

Carbohydrates—sugars and starches—are composed of the elements carbon, hydrogen and oxygen. Fats also are composed of these three elements. Proteins are made of four fundamental elements: carbon, hydrogen, oxygen and nitrogen.

The air is the principal source of nitrogen. Atmospheric nitrogen, however, cannot be used directly by most plants. The nitrogen must first be changed to either ammonia or nitrates, which plants then absorb through their roots. Ammonia consists of nitrogen and hydrogen; nitrates are compounds that contain nitrogen and oxygen.

Most ammonia and nitrates in the soil are produced by certain kinds of bacteria. Some of these bacteria, called *Rhizobium*, live on the roots of legume plants such as clover, alfalfa, beans and peanuts. The *Rhizobium* take nitrogen from air in the soil and combine, or fix, it into usable nitrogen compounds that are then absorbed by the legumes.

A similar relationship exists between a nitrogen-fixing species of blue-green algae and the water fern *Azolla pinnata*. Rice growers in Vietnam often add this combination of algae and fern to their fields. As some of the algae and fern die, bacteria in the wet fields break down their protein into simple nitrogen compounds that can be absorbed by the rice plants. The results: The fields produce up to twice as much rice as fields without the algae-fern combination.

Animals obtain nitrogen when they eat plants or other animals. They change the proteins in this food into proteins needed to build their own bodies. When the animals die, bacteria break down the proteins into compounds that can be used by plants.

Nitrogen can pass from the soil to organisms and back many times. Sometimes, it returns to the atmosphere. Organisms that return nitrogen to the atmosphere carry out a process called denitrification. Denitrifying bacteria break down ammonia and nitrates, releasing the nitrogen. This completes a complex series of events known as the nitrogen cycle.

is combined with carbon dioxide to form a simple sugar called glucose. The plants change some of the glucose into other carbohydrates (sugars and starches) and into more complex compounds such as proteins and fats. These are ultimately used by the plant for growth and energy.

Consumers

Consumers are organisms that depend on producers for food. All animals are consumers; they are unable to make their own food. Some consumers feed directly on producers. They are called herbivores. Grasshoppers, rabbits and deer are examples of herbivores.

Other consumers are carnivores. They feed on animals—either herbivores or other carnivores. Some carnivores are predators. Mountain lions, crocodiles and owls are predators. The animals they hunt are called prey. Other carnivores are scavengers—they feed on dead animals that they find. The carrion beetle eats rotting flesh; the larvae (young) of giant scarab beetles feed on rotting trees. The coyote is both a predator and a scavenger. It may chase and kill an animal itself, or it may eat the remains of another predator's dinner.

Some consumers feed on both plants and animals. They are called omnivores. Bluebirds, raccoons and foxes are omnivores. One of the most omnivorous of all animals is the brown rat. It eats insects, spiders, lizards, birds, fruits, vegetables, seeds, garbage and even other brown rats.

The ability to eat a variety of foods is a great advantage. If one food is scarce, the animal can eat something else. The grizzly bear is an omnivore that takes advantage of foods that are available only at certain times of the year. In spring, the grizzly eats mostly roots. In early summer, it eats horsetails and reed grass. In late summer, it feeds on berries and perhaps on salmon that it grabs out of swift-flowing rivers. And in all seasons, the grizzly chases ground squirrels.

Some animals eat plant matter during one stage of their lives and animal matter during another stage. Immature blister beetles eat other insects; adult blister beetles feed on plants. Newly hatched lobsters live among the microscopic life that drifts on the surface of the North Atlantic Ocean where they feed on tiny algae. Later, as adults, they live on the sea floor, scavenging or preying on various types of animals. Different habitats and diets mean that the two generations are not competing with one another for scarce resources.

Decomposers

The third major group of organisms—decomposers—feeds on wastes and the remains of dead plants and animals. Without decomposers, the Earth would soon be buried in dead bodies!

Fungi and bacteria are the main decomposers. As they break down the remains of dead organisms, they release carbon, nitrogen and other substances back into the environment to be used by producers to make new food.

Food Chains and Webs

On a prairie, the major producers are various kinds of grasses. Among the herbivores that feed on the grasses are mice. The mice are preyed on by carnivores such as snakes. The snakes are preyed on by hawks.

In a pond, the main producers are microscopic algae. These are eaten by herbivores such as water fleas. The water fleas, in turn, are eaten by small carnivores such as minnows. Larger carnivores in the pond, such as bass, feed on the minnows. The bass may become a meal for a bald eagle.

The arrangement of organisms based on who eats whom is called a food chain. Most organisms are part of more than one food chain. A deer feeds on many kinds of plants. A mountain lion may prefer deer, but it also preys on other mammals. A broad-winged hawk preys on a variety of birds, mammals and reptiles. This network, or combination of food chains, is called a food web.

WHAT'S IN A NAME?

Imagine this scenario: Several bird-watchers were walking through a swamp when they spotted a bird. "There's an anhinga," cried the first bird-watcher. "You're wrong, it's a darter!" said another. "No it's not, it's a snakebird," said the third. "It's a water turkey!" insisted yet another bird-watcher.

It is natural for people to give names to organisms. Problems arise, however, when different people give different names to the same organism. The four bird-watchers were all talking about the same bird. Imagine what might have happened if each of them had been walking alone when he or she saw the bird. When the four bird-watchers gathered later in the day to compare notes, it might have seemed as if they had seen four different kinds of birds.

To avoid this type of problem, every organism is given a scientific name. The name has two basic parts. The first part is its genus name, which is the general category to which the organism belongs. The second part is its species name, a more specific category to which only that kind of organism belongs. No two organisms that are different in structure share the same full scientific name.

The genus name for all anhingas is *Anhinga*. There are at least two species of anhingas, including *Anhinga rufa*, which inhabits tropical and temperate areas of Africa, Asia and Australia, and *Anhinga anhinga*, which lives in the Americas as far north as the southeastern United States.

How did these birds get their common names? *Anhinga* is based on a word from the Tupi language that is spoken by people who live in the Amazon River area of Brazil, where anhingas are often seen. The bird is called a darter by others because of the way it suddenly plunges, or darts, from low branches into the water to spear a fish. It is called a snakebird by some because of its long, serpentlike neck. Other people see it differently and call it a water turkey because of its big tail.

Most scientific names are based on two languages—Greek and Latin—once used by scientists in many countries. Like common names, scientific names often reflect features of an organism. White clover is *Trifolium repens*, meaning three-leafed creeper. The white oak is *Quercus alba*, meaning white oak. The Indian rhinoceros is *Rhinoceros unicornis*, meaning nose with one horn. All house cats are *Felis domestica*, meaning domestic cat. All humans are *Homo sapiens*, meaning intelligent man.

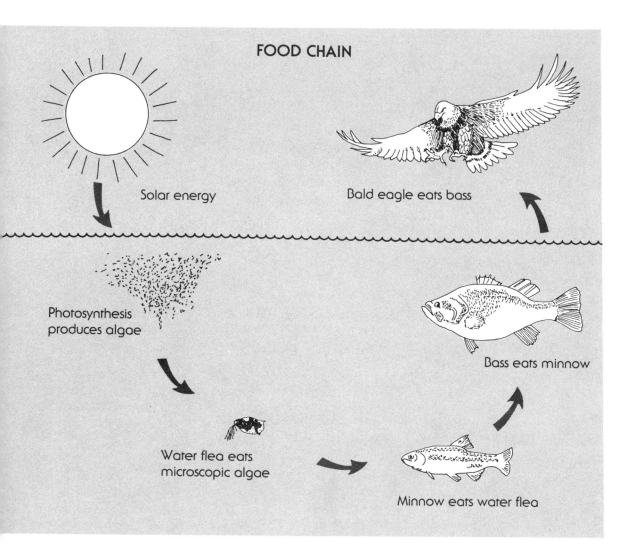

FOOD CHAIN

Solar energy

Bald eagle eats bass

Photosynthesis produces algae

Bass eats minnow

Water flea eats microscopic algae

Minnow eats water flea

All food chains and food webs begin with food producers. If the producers do not have the proper environmental conditions in which to grow and prosper, all the other organisms in the chain or web suffer. If a prolonged drought kills prairie grasses, there will be little, if any, food for the mice. Many of the mice will starve and die; they won't produce offspring. As the number of mice declines, snakes will go hungry; their numbers will also decline. This in turn will affect the hawks that prey on the snakes.

A Niche in the Community

Central Park lies in the middle of New York City, surrounded by busy streets, tall buildings and a large population of human beings. Within the park there also are many populations. To an ecologist, a population is a group of one kind of plant or animal that lives in a specific area. Central Park has populations of various types of trees, shrubs, small flowering herbs and grasses, plus mosses, lichens, ferns and algae. Many animal populations also live in Central Park. One survey of the park counted 269 kinds of birds, 9 kinds of fish, 6 kinds of bats, 3 kinds of woodchucks, 3 kinds of turtles and many other animals.

Every plant or animal population has a home, or place where it characteristically lives. This is the population's habitat. Central Park is the habitat of a population of azalea bushes. It also is the habitat of a population of pigeons. It provides all the things these organisms need to survive: sunshine, air, water and soil minerals for the azalea bushes; food, shelter, a place to rest and a place to reproduce for pigeons.

There are numerous kinds of habitats. The broadest kinds include forests, grasslands, deserts, tundra, oceans, rivers, ponds and swamps, all of which are discussed in the following chapters.

Some species have very broad habitats. Humans have made almost the entire planet their habitat. Houseflies also live in most parts of the world. Caribou roam over vast reaches of the arctic tundra. Cattails grow in marshes throughout temperate North America, Europe and Asia. Other species have very limited habitats. Lemurs live only on Madagascar. The Tiburon mariposa lily grows only on a small peninsula in California. White-winged guans are found only in forests in northwestern Peru.

All the organisms that live in a certain habitat form a community. They interact and affect one another in numerous ways, both directly and indirectly. Squirrels may prosper in a habitat because the habitat contains many oak trees that produce large crops of acorns. Pine martens thrive because

"Everything is connected to everything else."
–Barry Commoner,
The Closing Circle, 1971

BIRD BILLS

People use their hands to pick up food, carry bedding, clean their faces, comb their hair, feed their children, defend themselves and do dozens of other things. Birds do not have hands. They use their bills to perform these tasks.

Bird bills have evolved in various ways to meet specialized needs. For instance, different types of beaks are adapted to obtaining different kinds of food. Hawfinches have short, powerful bills that can crack open the hard seeds that make up their diet. The toucan has a long, saw-edged bill ideal for crunching fruit and berries. The crossbill has a pointed, twisted bill that enables it to pry open pinecones. The sword-beaked hummingbird is the only bird with a bill as long as its body; like other hummingbirds, it uses its bill to probe deep into flowers so that it can feed on nectar.

The monkey-eating eagle has a short, sharp, hooked bill—a perfect tool for ripping apart flesh. The long, swordlike bill of an anhinga can be used to spear fish, salamanders and crayfish. The merganser's bill is ridged with small toothlike serrations that help it grip prey such as fish and frogs. The shoveler duck has a comblike fringe along the edges of its broad bill that enables the duck to filter tiny plants and animals from water. The brown pelican has an expandable pouch in its lower bill that can hold three times as much food as the bird's stomach can hold.

there is a good supply of their food: squirrels. If gypsy moths invade the habitat and for several years eat the oak leaves, they kill or severely weaken the trees. This decreases the amount of food available for the squirrels. The squirrel population declines, and pine martens switch to other less-favored foods. They start eating berries, thus limiting the food available for certain birds in the habitat. The berry-eating animals help the plants disperse seeds. The seeds cannot be digested by the animals and are eventually excreted, usually at a distance from the parent plant. If conditions are favorable, the seeds will develop into new plants. When those plants flower, they will attract bees and other nectar-loving insects. Birds will find places among the branches in which to build nests.

Frequently, one community exists within another larger community. Worms and other organisms that live in the soil of a forest community make up a soil community. A rotting log on the forest floor may contain a community of insects, fungi, toads and other organisms. A cave within the forest may house a community of insects, bats and fungi.

Each population plays a unique role in a community. How that population fits into the community—what it does in the community—is called its niche. Mice eat seeds and hawks eat mice; they feed on different foods and thus have different niches in the same grassland community. In any community, no two types of organisms occupy the same niche. Only one population can occupy a particular niche. In a forest, both cardinals and indigo buntings eat seeds. But cardinals eat large seeds while the buntings eat small seeds.

Sometimes, two populations try to occupy the same niche. They compete for food or living space or nesting grounds or some other need. The species that is better fitted for the niche eventually crowds out the other species. In the 1890s an American bird lover imported 100 starlings from England and released them in Central Park. The starlings pushed native birds out of their nesting areas in the park; they prospered and multiplied. Today, there are millions of starlings in the United States, occupying niches once filled by other birds.

FOOD WEB

Life in the forest is a complex network of inter-dependence. Each plant or animal occupies a special place in the food web, relying on smaller organisms for food and in turn providing food for others in the web.

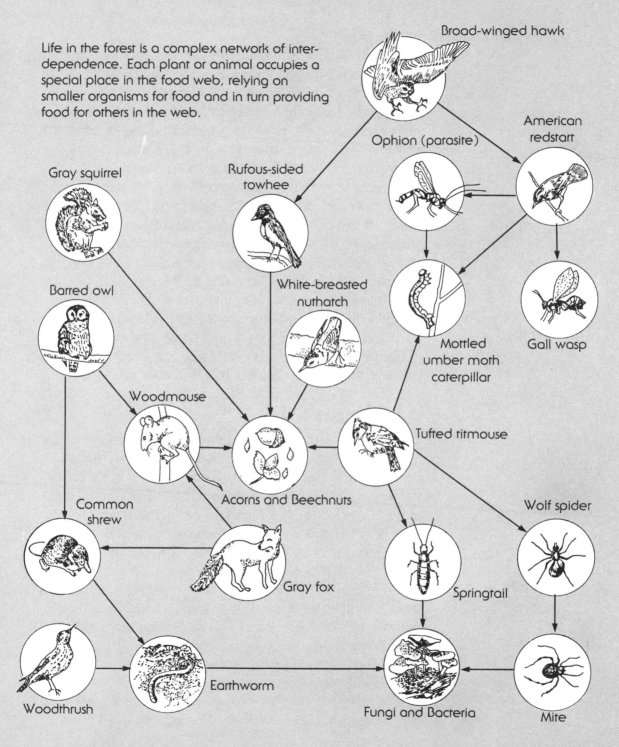

Broad-winged hawk

Ophion (parasite)

American redstart

Gray squirrel

Rufous-sided towhee

Barred owl

White-breasted nuthatch

Mottled umber moth caterpillar

Gall wasp

Woodmouse

Tufted titmouse

Common shrew

Acorns and Beechnuts

Wolf spider

Gray fox

Springtail

Woodthrush

Earthworm

Fungi and Bacteria

Mite

Ecosystems

The environment in which the Central Park community lives includes sunlight, air, water, rocks and minerals in the soil. These nonliving, or physical, parts of the environment are essential to the organisms. The birds indirectly take in the sun's energy when they eat seeds or fruit. They drink water and breathe in air. Some scratch in the soil, looking for worms and insects. Some build nests among the rocks.

A living community and its nonliving environment make up an ecosystem. Some ecosystems, such as Central Park, are small. Others, such as the Amazon rain forest, are large. None, however, is a closed, self-contained unit. Every ecosystem is affected by external factors. Pollutants produced by vehicles on nearby roads are inhaled by animals in Central Park. Human visitors trample grass and break tree limbs. Neighborhood cats wander into the park in search of unwary birds and mice.

Because almost no ecosystem is truly self-contained, many people refer to the entire Earth as one giant ecosystem.

Adaptations

Every organism has many adaptations that enable it to live efficiently in its environment. Some adaptations are structural—they are based on how the organism is built. Alfalfa plants have roots that grow downward 25 feet (8 meters) or more to reach water supplies far beneath the surface. Most cacti have very shallow root systems that may spread as much as 50 feet (15 meters) in all directions from the stem to quickly absorb scarce rainwater.

Other adaptations are functional—they are based on the ways in which the organism's internal systems operate. The manner in which organisms absorb oxygen is a functional adaptation. Elephants take in oxygen by breathing air into their lungs. Tuna absorb oxygen through their gills. Some frogs absorb oxygen through their moist skin.

Still other adaptations are behavioral—they are based on the things the organism does. The bittern hides from its enemies by standing absolutely still among marsh reeds. It points its long, slender bill upward to resemble one of the surrounding reeds.

Closely related species may be adapted to very different environments. The arctic fox lives near the North Pole while its relative, the fennec, lives in the deserts of northern Africa. One difference between the two species is their coats, which are colored to enable the foxes to blend into their surroundings. The arctic fox has a dark coat in summer, when the ground and shrubs are a mix of browns and greens. Then it grows a white coat for winter, when the environment is covered with snow. The fennec remains a light sand color— the color of the desert—all year.

Another difference between the two foxes is the size of their ears. The arctic fox has tiny ears; the fennec has huge ears. Many blood vessels are located near the surface of the ear, and heat passes from these blood vessels through the skin to the outside environment. The bigger the ears, the greater the animal's ability to lose heat. In the chilly Arctic, large ears would be a disadvantage—arctic animals need to conserve as much body heat as possible. In a hot desert, the reverse is true. There, large ears are an advantage because they help the animal get rid of excess heat.

Often, very different species may have similar adaptations that enable them to live in the same environment. Seals are mammals, yet their bodies are as streamlined as a fish's body. This enables the seals to move easily through their ocean habitat. Bats also are mammals, but they have developed wings that enable them to share the air with birds and insects.

Hibernation

The Canadian lynx lives in mountainous forests where winters are long and bitterly cold. It has long, thick fur that insulates the body and large feet that function as snowshoes. These adaptations enable the lynx to be active throughout the winter. Other creatures in their habitat, such as ground squirrels and chipmunks, become inactive as winter

ADAPTATIONS TO CLIMATE

Arctic Fox

Desert Fox (Fennec)

Closely related species may be adapted to very different environments. The arctic fox, for example, has tiny ears while the desert fox (fennec) has large ears that allow heat to pass through tiny blood vessels.

Santiago High School Library

MIGRATION ROUTES OF THE MONARCH BUTTERFLY

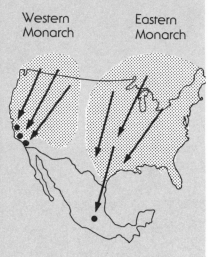

Western Monarch   Eastern Monarch

▨ Summer range

● Winter sites

Western monarch butterflies spend the summer months over a wide range. For winter, they migrate to warm sites in southern California. Eastern monarch butterflies also spend the summers over a wide range but migrate thousands of miles to warm sites in the mountains of south central Mexico.

approaches. They spend the winter months in caves or underground burrows where they enter a state of inactivity called hibernation. Their body temperature drops, their blood pressure falls, and their heartbeat and breathing rate slow down. Their bodies use much less energy than when they are active; the energy they do need comes from stored fat. When spring approaches and temperatures begin to rise, the animals come out of hibernation.

Estivation

Some animals escape the high temperatures of summer by going through a period of inactivity called estivation. In addition to saving energy, this enables the animals to conserve water. Pocket mice, turtles and frogs are animals that may estivate.

Migration

Another adaptation to seasonal changes is migration: the movement from one region to another and back. Animals migrate in order to have an adequate food and water supply, good breeding grounds and suitable temperatures. Monarch butterflies of North America feed only on milkweed plants. In summertime, monarchs are found as far north as southern Canada. In autumn, as temperatures drop and milkweed plants begin to die, the monarchs migrate southward. They spend the winter in specific groves of trees, huddling together in huge masses.

Humpback whales spend the summer months in polar oceans taking advantage of the season's rich food supply. In winter, they move to tropical waters. This is the time when their young are born.

The champion migrator is the arctic tern. Twice each year it flies from pole to pole—an annual round-trip of more than 11,000 miles (17,702 kilometers). The arctic tern nests within the Arctic Circle during July and August; then it flies to Antarctica, arriving in time for the southern summer. As fall approaches in the Southern Hemisphere, spring begins in the Northern Hemisphere, and the tern begins the long return journey to the Arctic.

Adapting to Change

Environments continually change. The change may be sudden, such as a forest fire or a flood. It may be slow, such as a gradual buildup of pollutants in a lake or a gradual rise in temperatures. If an organism is not suited to the change, it must either move to another environment, change or die.

Some organisms adapt by changing their behavior. When grasslands and marshes in California were turned into farms, the white-tailed kite's food supplies and habitats were destroyed, and the kite seemed headed for extinction. But then the kite learned to feed on the many insects and mice that live along the edge of the California freeways. It also found that the median strips that divide opposing lanes of traffic provide relatively safe nesting sites.

Structural and functional changes do not occur suddenly but require many generations, for they result from genetic variations among the members of a population. Certain species of English moths were originally light colored. This was a beneficial adaptation because the moths spent much of their time on tree trunks covered with light-colored lichens. The moths blended into the background, making them difficult to spot by hungry birds. As parts of England became industrialized, the air became filled with black smoke. Soot from factories covered the lichens on the tree trunks, turning them dark. Life became more difficult for the moths—now the birds could easily see them.

In any species, there is some variety. Most variations are neither helpful nor harmful. For the moths, however, variations in color did make a difference. Dark-colored moths now had a better chance of surviving than did their light-colored relatives. This meant they had a better chance to reproduce and pass on their dark coloring to their offspring. Gradually, dark-colored moths replaced light-colored moths in regions with high soot pollution.

The next major change occurred as factories began to limit the amount of pollution they produced. The English air became cleaner. Soot that washed off tree trunks was not replaced. New lichens were light colored. Today, once again, light-colored moths have an advantage.

MIGRATION ROUTES OF THE ARCTIC TERN

The arctic tern is one of the greatest long-distance migrators. Each year it flies from the North Pole to the South Pole and back, a round trip of more than 11,000 miles.

3

LAND HABITATS

There is an enormous variety in the habitats of the Earth. Indeed, no two habitats are exactly the same. The Amazon rain forest of Brazil is not identical to the rain forest on the Atlantic coast of Brazil. These two habitats have different environmental conditions and contain different species of plants and animals.

Because of the great variety among habitats, they can be categorized in only the broadest of terms. On land, the three major types of habitats are forests, grasslands and deserts. In addition, there are many other types, including chaparral, tundra and alpine.

A natural habitat does not have rigid boundaries. Both on land and in the sea, there is a gradual change from one type of habitat to another. For example, between a forest and a grassland, a woodland habitat is commonly found. Between an ocean and the beach, there is a tidal habitat that is alternately covered with water and exposed to the air. Many communities of plants and animals live in such transitional habitats.

To a large extent, two key factors determine the type of habitat that exists in a particular region. One factor is temperature. In a tropical rain forest, daytime temperatures are very warm throughout the year. In a temperate forest of western Europe, daytime temperatures are high in summer but often drop below freezing in winter.

Opposite page: The Earth's richest habitats are the tropical rain forests. A section of a few square miles can contain—on average—hundreds of species of trees, plants, mammals, birds, reptiles and amphibians.

Emergent tree

Canopy

Understory

Herb layer

Buttress roots

Forest floor

The second key factor is the availability of water. In a rain forest, water is plentiful; in a desert, water is scarce.

Forests

In a forest, the dominant food producers are trees. Trees require moisture throughout the year; they will die if the climate is dry for an extended period of time or if the soil does not contain a reserve of water. Fire must be rare. Also, populations of large herbivores must be small, to limit feeding on young trees.

Among the world's major forest habitats are tropical rain forests, temperate deciduous forests and northern evergreen forests.

Tropical Rain Forests

The Earth's richest habitats are the tropical rain forests. According to the U.S. National Academy of Sciences, a section of rain forest 4 square miles (10.4 square kilometers) in size typically contains about 750 species of trees, 750 species of other plants, 125 species of mammals, 400 species of birds, 100 species of reptiles and 60 species of amphibians.

Tropical rain forests are found in equatorial regions that receive plentiful rain throughout the year. The largest rain forest is in the Amazon River basin of South America. Others are found in Central America, the Congo River basin in Africa, India, southwestern Asia, the Philippines and northeastern Australia.

Continually warm temperatures, with little variation from season to season, allow growth all year long. Surprisingly, though, the soils of tropical rain forests are not very fertile. They contain relatively low concentrations of nutrients because the heavy rains leach, or wash out, the minerals. The rain forest trees have shallow roots. Many roots grow along the surface of the ground, pushing their delicate tips into the litter—the topmost layer of organic matter on the forest floor. As the litter is broken down by decomposers, nutrients are quickly absorbed by the tree roots.

The tops of the tallest trees in the rain forest form a dense layer called the canopy. This layer receives the greatest amount of sunlight, so it is here that most of the forest's photosynthesis takes place. Little sunlight penetrates to lower layers of the rain forest. This lack of sunlight restricts the growth of smaller trees, shrubs and ground plants, except along riversides where light penetration is good. In many places, the forest floor is bare except for a thin litter of leaves.

The trees of the rain forest generally have broad, evergreen leaves. The leaves at the top of the canopy, where sunlight is strongest, tend to be small. Lower in the forest, where there is less light, the plants have large, spearlike leaves to capture light from as broad an area as possible.

Epiphytes, including orchids and bromeliads, are common in lower parts of the canopy. Epiphytes are plants that grow upon other plants. They do not obtain nourishment from the supporting host plant; instead, they depend on their own roots, which can absorb water from the atmosphere and nutrients from debris that collects around them. Communities of insects, centipedes and even small frogs often live in the tangle of epiphytic leaves and roots.

Mosses, ferns and vines are plentiful. Some of the vines are parasites—that is, they obtain nourishment from other living things; their roots grow into trees and absorb food and moisture stored by the tree.

Animals are adapted to life in different layers of the forest. Numerous leaf-eating insects live in the upper part of the canopy. They attract insect-eating birds and spiders. The three-toed sloth is a mammal that spends its entire life in the canopy, never setting foot on the ground. Monkeys are also canopy dwellers, as is the fierce harpy eagle, which preys on both monkeys and sloths.

In lower trees—the understory of the forest—jaguars and other big cats crouch on branches, ready to drop onto ground-dwelling herbivores such as tapirs and peccaries. Elephants, small deer, rodents and many birds live on the ground, as do poisonous snakes such as the fer-de-lance and the bushmaster.

COLD BLOOD?

Birds and mammals are commonly called warm-blooded animals. They depend on metabolism (chemical processes within the body) to control their body temperatures, which remain relatively constant. Humans, for example, usually have a body temperature of 98.6° F (37° C).

Reptiles, amphibians and fish are said to be cold-blooded. No internal mechanism controls their body temperatures. Instead, their body temperatures change with the temperature of the environment. *Cold-bloodedness* is a misleading term, however. A lizard that has been lying in the sun may have a higher body temperature than a human.

Scientists use different terms to distinguish between the two groups of animals. Birds and mammals are homeothermic (same temperature), while other vertebrates are poikilothermic (varied temperature). Other terms are endothermic (inner temperature) and ectothermic (outer temperature). Birds and mammals are endothermic; that is, they use internal heat to keep their bodies warm. Reptiles, amphibians and fish are ectothermic—they depend on an external source, such as the sun, for warmth.

Temperate Deciduous Forests

In temperate climates of the eastern United States, western Europe and eastern Asia, there are large forests dominated by trees such as beech, oak, maple, hickory, walnut and basswood. Like the trees in the tropical rain forest, these trees have broad leaves. Unlike the tropical trees, however, these trees are deciduous—that is, they shed their leaves in the fall. As the masses of leaves are chewed by earthworms and decomposed by bacteria and fungi, huge amounts of nutrients are added to the soil, making it extremely rich. The shedding of the leaves also gives the habitat markedly different appearances during the four seasons of the year.

Temperate deciduous forests grow in regions that have hot summers and several months of cold winter weather. Although moisture is plentiful throughout the year, during cold weather the amount available to the trees is drastically reduced as water moves slowly in the soil and in the conducting tubes of plants. Since trees lose huge amounts of water through their leaves, they shed them to adapt to this winter water problem; without leaves, water loss is greatly reduced. In addition, freezing rain and heavy snow can break and otherwise damage broad leaves; this problem is limited in deciduous trees. Other natural adaptations that reduce the danger of winter damage include thick bark and waterproof scales on buds.

As temperatures rise in spring, the trees' buds begin to open, giving birth to new leaves. Prompted by sunlight reaching past the bare tree branches to the ground, a carpet of spring flowers forms on the forest floor. By the time a canopy of leaves overhead blocks out most of the sunlight, these small plants have completed much of their annual growth. Later, they are replaced by ferns and other plants that do not require as much light and so can survive beneath the dense canopy.

Animal life is not as abundant in the temperate deciduous forest as in the tropical rain forest, particularly in winter when vegetation is limited. Among the common herbivores are deer, rabbits, chipmunks, squirrels and beavers. Predators include bears, foxes and bobcats, as well as such birds as eagles, hawks and owls. Seed- and fruit-eating birds are abundant during the warmer months, but many of them migrate to escape the cold winter. So-called cold-blooded animals, such as frogs, salamanders, lizards and snakes, are common; they survive low winter temperatures by burying themselves in lake bottoms or moving into underground dens. Insects, also cold-blooded, generally survive the winter as eggs that hatch in early spring, just in time to feed on the new crop of tree leaves.

Northern Evergreen Forests

Across northern North America, Europe and Asia stretch vast expanses of forests. The primary trees are pines, firs, spruces and larches. The trees—called conifers—are very different from the evergreen trees of the tropical rain forest. Instead of flowers, conifers produce seeds in cones. Instead of broad leaves, they have needlelike leaves.

Larches shed their needles in fall, while other northern trees remain green throughout the year. A larch is shaped somewhat like a pyramid, with comparatively short branches near the treetop and the longest branches near the base. In winter, when the branches bend under the weight of heavy snow, the large lower branches support the smaller upper branches. Also, the pyramidlike shape causes much of the snow to slip off the branches and fall to the ground.

Precipitation is less than in more southern habitats. Winters are long and bitterly cold. Summers are short but warm enough to completely thaw the ground. The soil is generally acidic and soggy. Mosses are widespread, as are acid-loving plants such as cranberry, blueberry and wintergreen. Numerous streams cut through the forests and there are many lakes and ponds; along their edges deciduous trees such as birches and aspens may be found.

Migratory herbivores include moose and caribou, which move northward onto the tundra in the summer, and deer and elk, which spend the summer among the evergreens but move southward into deciduous forests during the winter. Smaller herbivores include squirrels and snowshoe hares; beavers are common near bodies of water where deciduous trees grow. Predators include wolves, bears, wolverines and martens. Migratory water birds and shorebirds are abundant during the summer, as are crossbills, whose twisted bills are adapted to remove seeds from the cones of the conifer trees. Insects, including the spruce budworm and other species that cause great damage to the trees, are numerous; but earthworms are seldom seen—they do not eat evergreen needles.

Grasslands

Almost every continent has major grasslands. These regions are referred to by different names around the world: There are the prairies of North America, the pampas of South America, the steppes of Asia, the savannas and velds of Africa.

Grasslands are commonly found in interior areas of continents where there are distinct wet and dry seasons, with drying winds and prolonged droughts. The dominant vegetation is grass, intermingled with sunflowers, legumes and other herbs. Shrubs and trees are scarce. These larger plants cannot survive long periods of drought; nor can they survive the fires that periodically sweep across the grasslands.

Fire plays an important role in grasslands ecology. Fire kills or severely damages large plants, but the grasses survive because many of their growing and reproductive structures are below ground. In addition, unlike leaves from other plants, grass leaves continue to grow from the base after being cropped off at the top. These characteristics are reasons why grass can be continuously eaten by herbivores. Stems in the soil continuously send up new shoots.

Grass plants have extensive root systems. Competition among species is limited because different species have roots that absorb water from different depths in the soil. Some species have short root systems that remove water only from the soil's surface layer. At the other extreme is alfalfa, which has roots that may extend more than 25 feet (8 meters) deep.

Grassland soil is usually very fertile. Earthworms, insects and rodents burrow in the soil, enabling water to seep into the ground and helping to ensure plentiful supplies of nutrients for the food producers.

Huge numbers of insects live in grasslands. Many are herbivores. They are preyed on by spiders, birds and mammals such as aardvarks and anteaters.

During periods of drought, when plant growth slows, many insects survive as eggs. Birds that feed on insects migrate. Herds of herbivorous mammals move to greener pastures where food and water are more plentiful. On the North American prairie, the major large herbivores are pronghorns. Antelopes dominate the African veld, wild asses and saiga antelopes roam the Asian steppe and kangaroos dominate the Australian grasslands. Predators and scavengers usually follow close behind the migrating herbivores.

Chaparral

Much of the western part of the United States is covered by dense thickets of evergreen shrubs. This habitat is called chaparral. The name comes from the Spanish word *chaparro*, which originally referred to dwarf evergreen oaks common in Mediterranean countries.

Chaparral is found from southern Oregon southward through California and into Arizona and Mexico. It does not form one continuous habitat. Rather, it occurs on numerous hillsides. Along the lower borders of a chaparral habitat are grasslands and sage scrub; along the upper, higher borders are coniferous forests.

Chaparral forms where winters are cool and moist and summers are hot and dry; almost all the rain falls in the winter months. The soil is usually rocky, low in nutrients and unable to hold much water.

Among the many species of shrubs are scrub oak, manzanita, sumac and mountain lilac. Most chaparral shrubs have small, thick, waxy leaves. Chaparral is very susceptible to fire because of the dry summers, growing piles of leaf litter and dense plants. Each year, large areas of chaparral burn. Although the shrubs are burned off, they soon reappear as new sprouts grow from underground root structures. The seeds, which are resistant to fire, germinate; in fact, the seeds of some species require the heat of fire for germination.

THE MALLEE FOWL

Parts of southern Australia are covered with semi-arid shrubland called mallee. Among the area's inhabitants is the mallee fowl. This bird does not incubate its eggs by sitting on them. Instead, a male and female work together to dig a deep hole. They fill the hole with a compost of wet twigs and leaves, which slowly decay and give off heat (the chemical reactions of decomposition cause a rise in temperature). The female lays her eggs in a chamber within the warm compost. The male then keeps the egg chamber at a constant temperature by adding compost to, or removing it from, the pile. When the young birds hatch, they must spend as much as 17 hours digging their way to the surface.

Lizards and snakes, numerous birds and a variety of mammals are among the animals of the chaparral. Herbivores include brush rabbits, California mice and mule deer; carnivores include gray foxes, pumas and rattlesnakes.

Habitats with environmental conditions and vegetation similar to the chaparral are found in many parts of the world, including around the Mediterranean Sea and in South Africa, Australia, China and Chile.

Deserts

Deserts occur in the southwestern United States, northern Mexico, along the west coast of South America, in much of northern and west-central Africa, in central Asia and in central Australia. Deserts are arid areas with scanty precipitation; many do not receive rain for several years at a time. Strong winds often produce violent dust storms. Daytime temperatures are high, at least during much of the year. Temperatures may vary greatly, however, within a 24-hour period. For example, temperatures at one oasis in the central Sahara Desert have ranged 100° F (55.5° C) within 24 hours: from a high of 126° F (52° C) during the day to a low of 26° F (–3° C) at night.

There are three main types of desert vegetation. Succulents, such as cacti and agaves, store water in their thick stems. Their leaves are modified into needlelike spines to reduce evaporation. Desert shrubs, such as sagebrush and mesquite, have small leaves covered with wax to reflect heat and limit water loss. Both succulents and shrubs have extensive root systems; the roots of the mesquite may grow to a depth in excess of 100 feet (30 meters). The roots of the night-blooming cereus may weigh as much as 85 pounds (38.5 kilograms).

The third type of vegetation is annual plants. Desert annuals, like all annuals, live for only one season. In the desert, however, annual species may complete their life cycles in only a few days. Following a brief period of rain, the annuals' seeds rapidly sprout, grow into plants, flower and produce seeds. The new generation of seeds lie dormant until the next rainfall.

Desert animals have various adaptations to conserve water. Many burrow into the ground during the hottest part of the day and are active only at night. Birds soar high into the cool upper levels of the atmosphere during the day and may migrate to avoid the hottest seasons. Eggs of amphibians and freshwater shrimp remain dormant, then hatch and quickly complete their life cycles when pools of water temporarily cover low-lying areas of the desert. Probably the most interesting desert mammal is the camel. In addition to being able to tolerate a wide range of body temperatures, it can safely lose about 30% of its weight in body water. Then, when it reaches a supply of water, it makes up this entire loss in a single drinking!

Desert-dwelling animals have numerous ways of adapting to their environment. Camels, for instance, are able to lose and gain almost a third of their weight in body water at one time.

Tundra

Encircling the Arctic Ocean north of the coniferous forests of North America, Europe and Asia is a treeless habitat called the tundra—a name derived from a Finnish word meaning "barren land." The tundra is characterized by frigid temperatures during most of the year. During the short, cool summer, the soil thaws to a depth of only a few inches; underneath is the permafrost—a layer that is permanently frozen.

Plant growth is slow because the growing season is short and because the soil is waterlogged and acidic. Some small shrubs, such as dwarf willows and birches, are present. Most of the plants, however, are grasses and other low, hardy perennials. Mosses and lichens are plentiful.

Caribou migrate to the tundra to feed during the short summer season. The caribou's major enemy, the gray wolf, is close behind. Moose and brown bears, which usually inhabit the neighboring forest, occasionally venture onto the tundra. Numerous birds also arrive for the summer months. All too soon, these animals will leave to avoid the long winter. The reindeer and wolves move back into the sheltering forests, as does the willow grouse. Some of the birds, however, undertake journeys of hundreds or even thousands of miles. For instance, many of the geese that visit the tundra during the summer spend the winter in Mexico or Africa.

Other animals, including small mammals such as arctic hare, lemmings, voles and ermines, live on the tundra all year. Larger year-round residents include musk ox and arctic fox. All these mammals remain active throughout the winter; hibernation is not possible because the frozen soil prevents construction of underground tunnels and burrows.

Many lakes, streams and bogs dot the tundra during the short period when temperatures rise above freezing. They provide ideal habitats for the larvae of mosquitoes and blackflies. After the larvae change (metamorphose) into adults, they form dense, vicious swarms. The mosquitoes and blackflies are bloodsuckers, and they attack any warm-blooded animal they find. Caribou try to put as much distance between themselves and the insects as possible by staying on higher, drier ground. The insect-eating birds, however, are delighted by the abundance of food.

CITIES: HABITATS OF PEOPLE

"People come to the city to find safety and happiness, to lead the good life," wrote the Greek philosopher Aristotle more than 2,300 years ago. Today, these words are still true for many people. Increasingly, however, cities provide neither safety, happiness nor the good life for many of their residents.

As the human population grows, towns turn into small cities, small cities become large cities, and large cities become megacities. As a city and its suburbs spread further and further outward, they eventually blend into other surburbs and cities. In the northeastern United States, the area from Boston to Washington, D.C., has been nicknamed Boswash. Boswash is a continuous urban area more than 600 miles (966 kilometers) long and from 30 to 100 miles (48 to 161 kilometers) wide.

The world's most populous city is Mexico City. It has more than 16 million residents—and the most polluted air of any major city in the world. Some 4.35 million tons of pollutants are released into the city's atmosphere each year, according to government statistics. Every day, 600 tons of disease-laden fecal dust enter the air from drying human and animal wastes. Every day, four tons of lead, which damages nerves and kidneys, enter the air, mostly from the exhaust of millions of cars that crowd the city's streets. Every day, huge amounts of ozone, which damages the lungs, fill the air, mostly as a result of chemical reactions of chemicals in auto exhausts. On the edge of the city, people live in shantytowns. Their homes are made of cardboard with aluminum roofs. There is no running water, nor are there any sewers; piles of garbage and human waste litter the area. The most common wildlife are rats, which roam everywhere.

The Mexican government has taken some steps to try to improve environmental conditions in Mexico City. It requires drivers to leave their cars at home one business workday each week. It replaced more than 3,500 smoke-belching city buses with models that burn cleaner fuel. It ordered the closing of the city's giant state-run oil refinery.

Meanwhile, the population of Mexico City continues to grow. So, too, does the population of other cities around the world, particularly in developing countries. According to a United Nations report, more than 85 countries had city populations that doubled between 1980 and 1990.

Mountain Habitats

Environmental conditions change with increasing altitude, or distance above sea level. Temperatures become cooler; the air becomes thinner and there is less oxygen; the winters are longer and more severe. As a result, there are usually several different habitats on a high mountain. Mount Washington, the highest peak in the northeastern United States at an altitude of 6,288 feet (1,917 meters), has three main habitats. The lower slopes of the mountain are covered with a deciduous forest. As altitude increases, the deciduous forest is replaced by a coniferous forest. Near the mountain's summit is an alpine habitat—grasses and low-lying plants grow there.

Mount Kenya, an extinct volcano in central Kenya, has an elevation of 17,058 feet (5,199 meters). At its base is a savanna with acacia trees and elephants. On the lower slopes, to an altitude of 5,500 feet (1,676 meters), is a rain forest dominated by huge tree ferns and where forest buffalo roam. This is replaced by a bamboo forest inhabited by small antelopes called duikers. At about 7,450 feet (2,271 meters), the bamboo gives way to scrub vegetation, with heath, groundsel and grasses; leopards prowl through this habitat. At 9,850 feet (3,002 meters), alpine grasses begin to predominate and small rock hyraxes scurry about. Finally, at about 12,000 feet (3,658 meters), the mountain becomes permanently covered with snow.

Even mountain snowfields show signs of life. Some species of small, wingless insects called grylloblattids live *only* on the snowfields of the Rocky Mountains. They feed on the frozen remains of lowland insects that were blown up onto the snowfields by winds. Many alpine plants are shaped like round cushions, an adaptation that protects against damage by the harsh winds. The leaves may be covered with transparent hairs that block air movement but admit sunlight. This adaptation enables the plant to form its own climate; temperatures within a cushion plant may reach 80° F (26° C), even though the air temperature around the plant is only 40° F (4° C).

Large herbivores may visit alpine meadows in spring and summer to feed on the growing plants. These animals are nimble and surefooted, able to climb along precipitous slopes. They include mountain goats, bighorn sheep, the European chamois and the American elk (wapiti). As winter approaches, these animals migrate downward, seeking shelter in the forests at lower altitudes. Large predators are scarce. So, too, are large birds. Only powerful fliers, such as the condor of the Andes, can handle the strong winds. Small birds are more common, but they stay close to the ground.

Species that live high on mountains may have very limited ranges. For example, condors, yellow-tailed woolly monkeys and spectacle bears are found only above elevations of 3,000 feet (914 meters) in the tropical Andes Mountains.

The Rain-Shadow Effect

Mountains often have one type of habitat on one slope and a considerably different habitat on the opposite slope. Mountains also affect habitats of surrounding lowlands. This occurs because mountain ranges affect rainfall distribution in a phenomenon known as the rain-shadow effect.

In Oregon, two mountain ranges run north to south, paralleling the Pacific coast: the Coast Range and, further inland, the higher Cascade Range. During much of the year, moist air moves onto land from the Pacific Ocean. As the air moves eastward, it meets the mountains and is forced to rise. When air rises, it cools and cannot hold as much moisture as warmer air. Thus, some of the moisture falls as rain or snow on the western slopes of the Coast and Cascade ranges. By the time the air has passed the peaks of the Cascades, it is quite dry. The average annual rainfall for the Oregon coast is about 80 inches (200 centimeters). On the high western slopes of the Coast Range, it averages as much as 130 inches (330 centimeters). East of the Cascades, annual rainfall is only about 12 inches (30 centimeters). As a result of this rain-shadow effect, plant and animal life in eastern Oregon is dramatically different than that in western Oregon. Sagebrush and grazing grasses are the dominant plants in the more arid parts of eastern Oregon, while forests and fertile, well-watered land suitable for agriculture cover much of western Oregon.

4
WATER HABITATS

On a warm, damp evening in late spring, male green frogs gather around a pond and fill the air with the sound of their courtship songs. Females, attracted by the songs, arrive at the pond and mating takes place. As the females expel eggs into the water, the males release sperm that fertilize the eggs.

The young animals that eventually hatch from these eggs look completely different than the adult frogs. Called larvae, or tadpoles, they have a fishlike shape with a flattened tail that is moved from side to side for swimming. They obtain oxygen they need by absorbing it from water through structures called gills. Their primary foods are microscopic algae and larger water plants.

Gradually, over a period of weeks, the larvae metamorphose (or change) into their adult form. Lungs develop, legs form, the tail is absorbed and many other changes occur. By the time these changes are completed, the animals are ready to move onto land. They take in oxygen through their lungs and switch to a diet of insects and other small animals. Even on land, however, the adult green frogs need to be surrounded by moisture. They live on damp forest floors and do not stray far from the ponds where they go to reproduce.

The green frog is among the organisms that depend on both land and water habitats for their survival. Just as a green frog cannot live in a desert or in certain other land habitats,

Opposite page: Measured by size, water habitats are the largest on Earth. Water habitats are usually separated into two types: freshwater, which includes lakes, ponds, rivers and streams; and marine, which includes oceans, bays, saltwater marshes and wetlands.

it cannot survive in every kind of water. Put a frog tadpole in an ocean, for example, and it will quickly die.

Just as the green frog moves between water and land, other organisms live part of their lives in one water habitat and another part of their lives in a different water habitat. Atlantic salmon leave the ocean to swim up freshwater rivers and breed in shallow, gravel-covered areas. After the fish lay their eggs, they return to the ocean. When the young fish hatch, they remain in the river from one to three years, until they are about 5 to 8 inches (12 to 20 centimeters) long. Then they swim downstream to the ocean, where they continue to grow and mature. They may travel hundreds of miles from their native rivers. Eventually, however, they will return to spawn in the same river where they were born.

The main nonliving factors that affect the types of organisms found in an aquatic, or water, habitat are the temperature, the amount of sunlight, the amounts of oxygen and carbon dioxide, and the amount of dissolved salts.

Aquatic habitats are usually separated into two types: freshwater and marine. In addition, on land and at the edge of oceans, there are habitats called wetlands.

Freshwater Habitats

Bodies of water that contain little salt and other dissolved minerals compose freshwater habitats. They range from huge lakes and long rivers to small springs and short-lived puddles. In tropical rain forests, freshwater habitats even exist high above the ground. Tree frogs lay their eggs in water that collects in tree holes or among the leaves of epiphytes.

Lakes and Ponds

Lakes and ponds form where fresh water fills depressions in the ground. Lakes are bigger and deeper than ponds. Some—like the Great Lakes of North America—have very deep areas not penetrated by sunlight.

Microscopic phytoplankton (simple plants; mainly one-celled) are important food producers in lakes and ponds. Life is most abundant in areas where sunlight reaches the bottom.

Here, grasses, water lilies and other rooted plants provide food as well as hiding places for animals.

The amount of plant nutrients dissolved in the water affects the diversity and abundance of organisms. The most productive lakes usually have a high content of nitrogen and other nutrients needed for plant growth. Near the surface, where photosynthesis takes place, oxygen levels are high. In deeper waters, where large amounts of dead algae and other organic matter are being decomposed, there is a shortage of oxygen. Carp and catfish are common bottom-dwellers in these lakes.

Lakes that contain low levels of plant nutrients are relatively unproductive. Because there is comparatively little plankton and suspended matter, the waters are clear. However, oxygen is plentiful. Bottom-dwelling fish such as lake trout live in these lakes.

Lakes and ponds are generally closed habitats—most of the soil and other material carried into these lakes or ponds stays there. The basin gradually fills up. It becomes a marsh and eventually dry land. As the lakes and ponds change with time, so does the type of life that they can support.

Rivers and Streams

Rivers and streams are bodies of flowing water. They carry fresh water from an area of land called a watershed to either a lake or an ocean. Unlike lakes and ponds, rivers and streams are open habitats—they do not accumulate water or minerals but carry them steadily downstream.

The word *river* is usually used to describe a body of water that is comparatively deep and warm, with a bottom that is covered with silt and mud. In contrast, the word *stream* refers to flowing water that is cool and shallow, with a bottom of gravel, stones or boulders. There are many exceptions to these definitions. For instance, the Mississippi River at its upper reaches has all the characteristics of a stream.

Seasonal variations are common in many rivers and streams. Water volume may greatly increase following heavy rains or the melting of snow. During periods of drought, water flow

THE DRIFTERS

The largest group of organisms in most aquatic habitats, in terms of numbers, are the plankton. Plankton are organisms that float and drift on or near the surface of the water; most are very small.

Food-producing plankton, or phytoplankon, consist of various kinds of microscopic algae. Most aquatic food chains begin with phytoplankton. Animal plankton, or zooplankton, include microscopic protozoans, tiny crustaceans called copepods and the larvae of many kinds of fish and other larger animals. Zooplankton are the primary herbivores in aquatic habitats.

may slow to a trickle. Many organisms have life cycles adapted to these variations.

The speed at which the water flows is another important factor in determining which organisms are present. Plankton are generally not found in free-flowing rivers because they are quickly carried downstream. Fast-flowing water contains more dissolved oxygen than slow-flowing water. Many organisms that live in fast-moving water have adaptations that enable them to cling to rocks. Organisms that live in the sediments of slow-flowing rivers do not have clinging adaptations, but they may have exceptionally large gills to enable them to obtain enough oxygen.

Marine Habitats

The five oceans compose the major marine, or saltwater, habitats. The largest is the Pacific Ocean; the others are the Atlantic, Indian, Antarctic and Arctic oceans. Most seas also contain salt water; they generally are part of the larger oceans. For example, the Caribbean Sea is a western branch of the Atlantic Ocean, and the Bering Sea is part of the Pacific Ocean between Alaska and Siberia. The Bay of Fundy, which separates Nova Scotia and New Brunswick, is an arm of the Atlantic Ocean. The Persian Gulf connects to the Gulf of Oman, which opens into the Indian Ocean.

Environmental factors vary greatly from place to place. The chemical and physical conditions of the water are critical in determining the kinds of organisms found in certain parts of the ocean.

Among the most significant environmental factors is salinity—the amount of salt dissolved in the water. Typically, ocean water has a salinity of 35 parts per thousand. That is, a 1,000-gram sample of the seawater contains 35 grams of salt. In places where rivers empty into an ocean, however, the salinity is lower because the incoming fresh water contains very little salt. In parts of the Baltic Sea fed by large rivers, salinity may fall below 10 parts per thousand at certain times of the year. Elsewhere, particularly in warm seas where there is very little precipitation and a lot of evaporation, salinity is high. In some lagoons along the Texas coast, salinity has reached 100 parts per thousand during hot summers.

Another important environmental factor is the amount of carbon dioxide, oxygen and other gases in ocean water. These gases tend to be more abundant near the surface, for two reasons: First, atmospheric gases dissolve in surface waters; second, oxygen-producing phytoplankton live near the surface where there is sunlight for photosynthesis.

Water temperatures are highest in surface waters. At a depth of 33 to130 feet (10 to 40 meters), there is a transition zone where the temperature drops rapidly. Beneath, in the deep zone, the temperature is usually just above freezing.

Pressure increases with depth because of the weight of the overlying water. At the bottom of the deepest parts of the oceans, pressure is 1,000 times as great as the pressure at the surface.

The ocean floor is as varied in its physical features, or topography, as any continent of land. Nowhere on Earth are there taller mountains, deeper canyons or larger plains than

UNDERWATER GARDENS

Coral reefs look like colorful underwater gardens, but these habitats are built by billions upon billions of tiny animals called corals. These animals look much like jellyfish, to which they are related, but corals are much smaller. Many corals are about the size of the period that ends this sentence. A few are larger than a pea. They feed on zooplankton, catching the tiny animals with tentacles armed with deadly stinging cells.

Cells in the outer layer of a coral's body remove dissolved calcium salts from the seawater and use it to create a hard limestone cup around the sides and bottom of its body. The cup cements the coral to the reef and provides the animal with shelter and protection.

Corals require relatively warm water for survival. Thus coral reefs are most common in tropical and subtropical seas. Corals also need sunlight for one-celled algae that live within their bodies. The relationship between the corals and the algae is a good example of symbiosis—a relationship in which both species benefit. As the algae carry out photosynthesis, they make food both for themselves and for their coral hosts; they also provide the corals with oxygen. In return, the algae get carbon dioxide from the corals, plus a protective home.

The diversity of life in coral reefs rivals that of tropical rain forests. A single reef may be home to as many as 3,000 species of animals. Among the most noticeable are the swarms of brilliantly colored fish, with wonderful names like damselfish, parrot fish, cowfish, butterfly fish and neon gobies.

beneath the oceans. In some places, the ocean floor is sandy. Elsewhere it is covered with mud and silt.

Movements of ocean water also influence habitats. Surface currents transport huge volumes of water over great distances. The Gulf Stream, a current that carries warm water northward along the eastern coast of North America, is 90 miles (145 kilometers) wide and more than 6,600 feet (2,012 meters) deep in some places.

Waves have a major effect on ocean habitats when they break and hit the shore; so do tides, which cause the water level along shorelines to alternately rise and fall.

Life in the Sea

The food producers of marine habitats are almost exclusively algae. One-celled algae are major producers; seaweeds, which are large multi-celled algae, are important in some marine habitats. Off the coast of California, for example, lie underground forests of giant kelp. Near Bermuda, in the North Atlantic, is an area called the Sargasso Sea, rich with a floating seaweed called sargassum.

In the tropics, levels of photosynthesis are high year-round. Closer to the poles there are seasonal variations, with the highest food production occurring in spring and fall. Many animals migrate, following this food supply, according to these variations.

Marine zooplankton include the larvae of oysters, worms and many fish that spend their adult lives as active swimmers or living on the ocean bottom. Most of the zooplankton, however, consist of small crustaceans. Among these are shrimplike animals called krill. They are among the giants of the planktonic world, though they usually are less than 2 inches (5 centimeters) long. Despite their small size, they are the primary food of the blue whale, the largest animal ever to live on Earth.

Marine animals that are active swimmers and able to move freely through the water are called nekton. Fish, squid, sea snakes, sea turtles, whales and seals are examples of nekton. They are almost exclusively carnivorous. Some are solitary animals; others, such as herring, swim in large groups called schools.

Most nekton live near the surface or in twilight waters, but some species live thousands of feet below the ocean's surface in a habitat of eternal darkness. Food is scarce in this region so the animals have evolved an amazing array of features to help them capture food. Some deep-sea fish have huge, gaping mouths that enable them to eat prey larger than themselves. Other species have bioluminescent (light-producing) organs that can be flashed on and off to attract prey.

BETWEEN LAND AND SEA

Places where tides alternately cover and expose shorelines are called intertidal zones. Some of these places are sandy beaches; others are grassy and muddy; still others are rocky. Each has its own community of inhabitants. These organisms have adapted to living part of each day underwater and part of it exposed to air. Barnacles, for example, cement themselves to rocks, so that moving waters do not carry them away from their habitat. While the tide is in, the barnacles open their shells to absorb oxygen and obtain food. As the water recedes, the barnacles close their shells. This seals in enough water to prevent drying and allows them to survive until the tide advances again.

Among the varied habitats of intertidal zones is the tide pool. During low tide on a rocky beach, most of the rocks are out of water; but here and there along the beach are depressed areas that trap water, retaining it while the rest of the beach is exposed to the air. These are the tide pools. Though they may be as small as a soup bowl, they are filled with life. In addition to microscopic algae, there are various seaweeds attached to the rocks. Tiny shrimp, baby crabs and small fish find protection among the strands of seaweed. Snails graze on the plants, scraping the vegetation off the rocks with their rough tongues. A snail called a drill uses its sharp tongue to drill a hole through a mussel's shell, then eats the mussel through the small hole. Starfish wrap their arms around a clam's shell and pull it apart to get at the meat. Sea anemones, often brightly colored in shades of red and purple, look like flowers but they are animals. Their "petals" are tentacles that wave enticingly, then quickly grab and sting any small animal that comes too close.

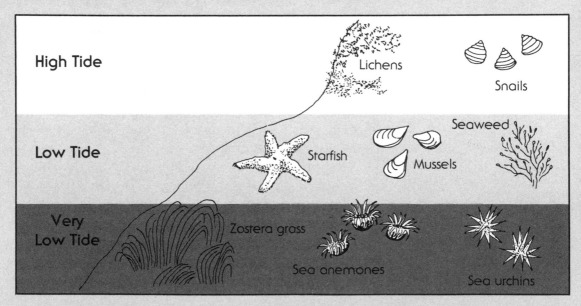

High Tide — Lichens — Snails

Low Tide — Starfish — Mussels — Seaweed

Very Low Tide — Zostera grass — Sea anemones — Sea urchins

Animals that live on or in the ocean floor are called benthos. They include sponges, worms, sea urchins, starfish, clams, barnacles and crabs.

Birds also are an important part of ocean habitats. Gannets, frigate birds and cormorants dive into the water to capture fish; skimmers scoop food from the surface; auks and penguins "fly" underwater in pursuit of prey.

Wetlands

Wetlands are areas that are regularly saturated by water, with vegetation that can live in saturated soil conditions. Swamps, marshes, bogs and tidal flats are examples of wetlands. Some wetlands form inland and contain fresh water. Other wetlands exist in coastal areas and contain salty or brackish water.

Single-celled algae make significant contributions to the wetland food supply. The primary food producers, however, are green plants: papyrus in an African freshwater swamp, bulrushes in Spain's vast Coto Doñana, mangrove trees in Hawaii, cordgrass in North America's Chesapeake Bay. Leaves that are not eaten by animals eventually die and fall into the water, where they become part of other food chains and are decomposed by bacteria.

Until recently, the importance of wetlands was not fully appreciated. Many people considered them wastelands because they were breeding grounds for mosquitoes and other pests and because they were unsuitable for building and farming. But wetlands are among the most valuable habitats on Earth. They provide homes for a great variety of animals—including many valued fish species for whom mosquito larvae are an important source of food. Wetlands are breeding and feeding areas for millions of ducks and other water birds; during their long migrations, these birds stop to rest in wetlands along the way.

Reptiles are common wetland inhabitants, particularly in tropical and subtropical regions. They include crocodiles, alligators, snakes, lizards and turtles. Frogs and other amphibians are numerous. Mammals include muskrats and mink in North American wetlands, capybaras in South American swamps, and huge hippopotamuses in Africa's papyrus swamps.

Many coastal wetlands form in river estuaries, where fresh water flowing downstream merges with the ocean's salt water. In these transitional zones, there is a wide range of salinity. Salt levels are low upstream, then gradually rise as the water gets closer to the open ocean. Salt levels fluctuate seasonally and with precipitation. Rivers usually carry their greatest loads of fresh water in springtime, following spring rains and the melting of winter snows. As this mass of fresh water flows into the estuary, the water in the estuary becomes less salty. During the comparatively dry summer months, rivers carry less fresh water and salt levels in the estuary water rise.

Another fluctuation of salinity occurs as tides ebb and flow. Twice each day, the tides carry salt water up the estuary, raising water levels; twice each day, the tides retreat, leaving some habitats temporarily exposed to the air. The area affected by the tides may be enormous. Tides carry salt water from the Atlantic Ocean some 60 miles (97 kilometers) up the Connecticut River—and 600 miles (966 kilometers) up the Amazon River!

Some organisms, such as the Atlantic oyster, can tolerate a wide range of salinity; they may be found in numerous habitats along an estuary. Other organisms are less adaptable, and thus their distribution is more limited. For example, the Atlantic oyster's main predator, the oyster drill, requires a salinity of at least 15 parts per thousand. Thus, Atlantic oysters living in the waters with salinities less than 15 parts per thousand have a better chance of survival than their relatives in saltier waters.

Most rivers carry large quantities of sand, silt and other sediments. As the rivers approach the sea, they slow down and sediment settles to the bottom. Plant stems and roots trap and hold some of the sediment, creating habitats for many kinds of organisms.

A single acre of wetland in a healthy estuary contains millions of invertebrate animals, including various types of crabs, snails, clams and oysters. Some live in habitats that are always underwater. Others are adapted to being alternately exposed to air and covered with water. Fiddler crabs scuttle sideways along exposed mud flats, consuming algae and other food particles in the mud. They, in turn, are eaten by raccoons and some of the many birds that live among the grasses.

As the tide comes in, the fiddler crabs crawl into burrows they have dug beneath the cordgrass. Some of these burrows may be 2 feet (0.6 meter) deep. To prevent water from flooding and destroying the burrows, the crabs make doors from mud that they have rolled into little pellets. The crabs remain in their burrows until the tide recedes.

Some fish, such as white perch, spend their entire lives in estuaries. Other fish come to reproduce—they mate and lay eggs, then return to the sea. In the estuaries, their young have a plentiful food supply in a habitat where they are safe from some of their ocean enemies.

Incoming tides bring large ocean fish in search of food. As the tides ebb, the fish return to the sea. Ebbing tides also flush the wetlands, carrying out decaying plant leaves, sediment, dissolved salts and other transient material.

Wetlands are nurseries and spawning grounds for oysters, shrimp, crabs and many fish, including flounder, bluefish, sea trout and striped bass. Up to 90% of the animals in commercial fish catches in the United States started life in the wetlands. Wetlands are also critical habitats for many plants and animals listed as endangered or threatened. In the United States, these organisms include the pondberry, Florida panther, manatee, whooping crane, Everglade kite and Schaus swallowtail butterfly.

5

CHANGING THE ENVIRONMENT

 When Hurricane David smashed into the island of Dominica on August 29, 1979, it destroyed one of the Caribbean's most extensive rain forests. Lush, green mountainsides were turned into barren, muddy graveyards as the storm's fierce winds snapped trees as if they were matchsticks.

Another large forest habitat was destroyed the following year, when Mount St. Helens, in the state of Washington, erupted. A blast of heated gas shot out of the volcano, blowing down the coniferous trees within approximately 5 miles (8 kilometers) of the mountain's north flank. Farther away, many thousands of additional trees were either blown down or scorched and killed by the heat. Almost all animal life in the area was killed.

Natural events such as storms, volcanic eruptions, earthquakes and fires caused by lightning have always brought chaos. Sometimes the effects have been truly cataclysmic. During the ice ages, thick sheets of ice from the Arctic advanced over the land and covered much of North America, Europe and Asia. The ice molded valleys and created lakes, changing the surface of the land in many ways. Rapidly changing temperatures and other climatic disruptions associated with the ice ages triggered the extinction of numerous plant and animal species.

Opposite page:
Natural environments can be disturbed by a number of natural events, including hurricanes, volcanoes, earthquakes, drought, flooding and pests. The most destructive habitat destroyers of all, however, are humans.

Nature's power to change the environment has been rivaled and, in many ways, surpassed by the activities of human beings. People may not knock down trees in a forest as rapidly as a hurricane or a volcanic eruption, but each year people cut down many more forests than are destroyed by natural events. Bulldozers and other heavy construction equipment may seem tiny beside an ice-age glacier, but they are equally effective at leveling hills, channeling rivers and filling wetlands.

Reshaping the Earth

At its height, the road system of the ancient Roman Empire consisted of 53,000 miles (85,293 kilometers) of roads. To-day, the United States has more than 3.8 million miles (6.1 million kilometers) of roads. It also has railroad lines, airports and canals. All these structures are designed to aid the transport of people and their belongings. All take up enormous amounts of land.

Roads and other transportation structures are just one kind of construction that replaces natural habitats with artificial habitats. Housing developments, shopping malls, vacation resorts, schools, hospitals, gas stations, sports stadiums, restaurants—the list goes on and on. They all provide benefits, but they also adversely affect the natural environment.

For example, large rivers all over the world have been dammed to retain water for irrigation, drinking supplies, electric power generation and flood control. Vast areas of land are permanently buried beneath the waters of the reservoirs behind these dams. The Aswan High Dam, which blocks the Nile River in Upper Egypt, created a reservoir that is an average of 6 miles (10 kilometers) wide and extends 310 miles (499 kilometers) upstream. The Tucuruí Dam on the Tocantins River in Brazil flooded more than 850 square miles (2,201 square kilometers) of rain forest.

When the first European settlers arrived in North America, there were more than 200 million acres (81 million hectares) of wetlands in the area that today forms the 48 contiguous American states. By 1990, about 95 million acres (38 million hectares) remained, and the country continues to lose several hundred thousand acres a year. The great majority of wetland loss in the United States has resulted from agricultural practices—wetlands have been drained for farmland on which to grow wheat and other crops. Historically, drainage for agriculture has accounted for about 80% of all freshwater wetlands lost.

Agriculture has also replaced almost all of the native grasslands in the United States. In grassland areas where the climate is too dry for crops, domestic animals are raised. Native herbivores are replaced with cattle, sheep and goats. Here, as on croplands, native species are often regarded as pests because they compete with animals raised by humans. Wolves, birds, rodents, insects and numerous kinds of plants are killed, using methods ranging from shotguns to chemical pesticides. Such activities often take place on public lands, with the approval and guidance of government agencies.

Deforestation

At the beginning of the 1990s, the world's forests were being cut at a rate of 80 acres (32 hectares) a minute. Each year, 40 million to 50 million acres (16 to 20 million hectares) are destroyed—an area about the size of the state of Washington. The forests are being cut primarily for their wood, but large areas are also being cleared for farms or to extract gold and other minerals.

In some places, trees are cut selectively, meaning that only certain trees are cut leaving the rest of the forest intact. Most commercial operations, however, use a method called clear-cutting in which large sections of a forest are completely cleared of vegetation.

The world's forests are being cut down much faster than they are being replaced. Even if they are replanted with seedlings, it will take many generations of undisturbed growth before the new habitats will support the previously rich variety of organisms. Some forest habitats, particularly rain-forest habitats, can never be recreated because once they are gone, the conditions needed to form them no longer exist.

OLD-GROWTH FORESTS

Ancient forests of towering firs, hemlocks, cedars and spruce once covered about 70,000 square miles (180,300 square kilometers), from the tip of the Alaska panhandle through Canada south into northern California. Logging has severely reduced these forests: About 40% of Canada's Pacific forests remain; less than 10% of the U.S. forests remain.

Forests support a rich variety of birds, deer, bats, flying squirrels and other animals. The ground is densely covered with mosses, ferns and debris, which prevent erosion of sediment into streams that flow through the forests. As a result, the streams contain exceptionally clean water, making them ideal habitats for salmon and trout.

No laws protect endangered ecosystems. The United States, however, has laws that protect the habitats of endangered species. Environmentalists depend on these laws as they work to save the old-growth forests of the Pacific Northwest.

One species whose future is threatened by the destruction of the old-growth forests is the northern spotted owl. This bird nests only in dead, but still-standing, trees called snags. Snags are common only in old-growth forests; in fact, they are one of the basic characteristics of these forest habitats.

Most loggers do not selectively cut trees from the forests of the Pacific Northwest. Rather, they use a method called clear-cutting, which topples everything that stands. When they finish, only masses of debris cover the ground.

Because of clear-cutting, the northern spotted owl's habitat has been severely reduced and its population has reached critically low levels. Throughout the 1980s, environmentalists used the owl's plight in their efforts to save the forests. Finally, in 1990, the U.S. government declared the owl a threatened species. This required the government to prepare a plan to limit logging and provide protection for the bird.

Recovery of Minerals and Energy

Metals, other minerals and fossil fuels (coal, oil and natural gas) are not distributed evenly throughout the Earth's surface. Rather, they are concentrated in accumulations called ore deposits. Various mining and drilling operations are used to recover these ores. For example, some coal deposits lie near the ground's surface and are recovered by a type of mining that must be preceded by stripping away any overlying soil. Other coal deposits lie deep under the surface; tunnels are needed to reach these deposits. Petroleum (oil) is recovered by drilling into deposits, then bringing up the petroleum through pipes.

During recovery, large tracts of land are disturbed. For example, extracting ore can create billions of cubic feet of leftover rocks and soil, called tailings. These are piled to form hills, dumped into wetlands or disposed of in some other way that destroys habitats

Recovery is only part of the story. To get minerals and energy from their sources to their point of use, additional development is generally needed. In Alaska, oil is being recovered from fields on the North Slopes. To get this oil to an ice-free port so that it can be shipped to users, a pipeline 800 miles (1,287 kilometers) long was built across the Alaskan tundra. In addition, 12 pumping stations and a huge tanker terminal in the port city of Valdez were built.

In Hawaii, there is a proposal to build a series of geothermal power plants on the island of Hawaii (the Big Island). Heat from the island's volcanoes would be used to generate electricity. This electricity would then be transported via cables across the island, across the bottom of the ocean to the island of Maui, across Maui, again across the ocean bottom, and finally to customers on the island of Oahu. Where the cables would cross land, rain forests would be destroyed. Along the sea floor, coral reefs would be destroyed. Large amounts of land would also be altered by the 150 to 200 geothermal wellheads, the power plants, the cooling towers, roads and other related structures.

Many substances must be processed before they can be used. For example, after iron ore is mined, the metal must be separated from the other materials in the ore. It is then processed to make iron and steel products. Smelters, blast furnaces, rolling mills and other structures that produce pollution are part of this process.

Polluting the Earth

"We have laid waste to our soils and the rivers and the forests that our forefathers bequeathed to us," said Vaclav Havel, playwright and president of Czechoslovakia, in 1990. Havel was speaking about his homeland, but his words are appropriate throughout the world. Everywhere people are polluting the Earth with their wastes.

Pollution can be defined as the introduction of something into the environment that harms the environment or its organisms. Pollutants include chemicals, radiation, noise and heat. For example, when a factory discharges large amounts of hot water into a cold river, the river becomes polluted; pollution by heat is called thermal pollution. Fish and other organisms in the river cannot adapt to the higher temperatures and they die.

Pollutants can be solids, liquids or gases. Solid wastes range from household garbage and medical wastes to mine tailings and soot that pours out of chimneys. Liquid wastes include sewage from homes and factories, plus chemical-laden waters that run off lawns, golf courses and farmlands. Gaseous wastes pour into the atmosphere from fires, factory smokestacks and the tailpipes of motor vehicles.

The amount of wastes produced is humongous, especially in industrialized countries. Each year, for example, Americans discard 160 million tons of garbage—more garbage than any other country in the world, including China, which has four times as many people.

Once the pollutants enter the environment, they may remain for years before being broken down into harmless substances. Twenty years after the barge *Florida* ran aground off the Massachusetts coast in 1969 and spilled oil into the marine waters, traces of the oil were still present in wetland sediments and in the tissues of animals.

Populating the Earth

Construction, deforestation, mining, pollution: These and other human activities that destroy natural habitats are fed by the needs and demands of people. All these activities are increasing because the number of people on Earth is increasing.

The rate at which any population of organisms grows reflects the difference between the population's birth rate and its death rate. If the birth rate is greater than the death rate, the population grows. If the birth rate is less than the death rate, the population declines. Despite disease epidemics, famines, wars and other catastrophies, people have produced babies faster than people have died. As a result, the world's human population has steadily increased.

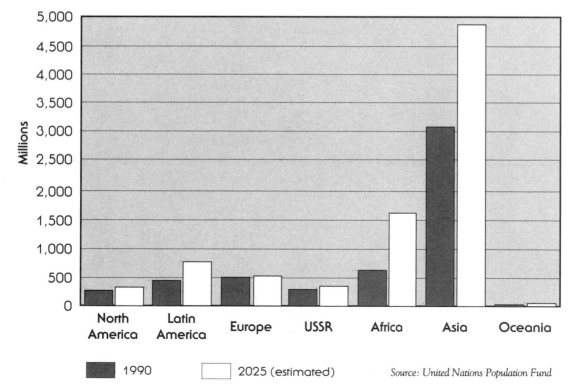

WORLD POPULATION

■ 1990   □ 2025 (estimated)

Source: United Nations Population Fund

During the first two million years of human history, the total population probably never exceeded 10 million. It wasn't until the Stone Age, less than 10,000 years ago, when people domesticated animals and developed agriculture, that the human population began to increase more rapidly. By the year A.D. 1, there still were only 250 million people on Earth. It took until 1650 for this population to double to 500 million. Since then, the population has increased at an ever-faster pace. The population reached 1 billion around the year 1830, 2 billion in 1930, 3 billion in 1960 and 4 billion around 1975.

By mid-1991, there were 5.4 billion people on Earth. Every second, 3 more babies were born. Every day, there were a quarter of a million births. Every year, there were an additional 90 million to 100 million people—people who needed food, clothing and shelter.

By the year 2001, world population is projected to be 6.4 billion. By 2025, it will reach 8.5 billion. For the foreseeable future, according to the United Nations Population Fund, 95% of this growth will be in developing countries, particularly in southern Asia and Africa but also in Arab countries and in Latin America and the Caribbean.

"These increasing numbers are eating away at the Earth itself," noted Nafis Sadik, executive director of the United Nations Population Fund, in a 1990 report. "Developed or developing, the more people the more pollution: at any level of development larger numbers consume more resources and produce more waste."

Introducing Plants and Animals

Sometimes people introduce a new organism into an environment. This may occur accidentally: Rats that stow away on a ship in one port may disembark at a port on another continent halfway around the world. Or the introduction may be deliberate: People imported English sparrows into the United States hoping that the birds would attack the canker-worm, an insect that was causing much damage to desirable shade trees.

Introduced species are called exotics. Usually, exotics cause more harm than good. They upset the delicate balance that exists within the environment.

Introduction of Sparrows

English sparrows introduced into the United States during the 1850s and 1860s thrived and extended their range. They were successful for several reasons. They can live in a wide variety of habitats, including cities, suburbs and farming areas. They eat a wide variety of food. They have a high birth rate. A female nests at least twice and perhaps as many as five times a year and each time she produces four to seven fledglings, all of which usually survive. The sparrows are aggressive animals and monopolize food supplies, driving off other birds that try to feed. They take over the nesting sites of barn swallows, house wrens and other birds. They may even destroy these birds' eggs, leading to population declines in the native species.

By the 1880s, Americans realized that the importation of English sparrows had resulted in, at best, mixed blessings. Any benefits were offset by the high environmental cost of introducing the birds. Some states passed laws designed to eliminate the sparrows, but it was too late. The sparrows were in the United States to stay.

A Plague of Rabbits

In the 1800s, European settlers in Australia imported a few rabbits from their homeland. Free of natural predators, the rabbits multiplied at a phenomenal rate. Rabbits feed mainly on grasses, and they were soon causing an enormous amount of damage not only to natural habitats but also to crops and sheep pastures.

Shooting, poisoning and other tactics were used to try to lower the rabbit population and to prevent their spread. The Australian government even built a fence some 1,000 miles (1,609 kilometers) long, running north to south through the country, in an unsuccessful attempt to keep the rabbits out of western Australia.

KILLER CROCODILES

One of the most ferocious of all animals is the Nile crocodile, which inhabits rivers, lakes and swampy areas throughout tropical and southern Africa. This aggressive predator can grow to 21 feet (6.4 meters) in length and weigh more than a ton. Nile crocodiles have little difficulty catching large animals such as antelope, zebra and warthogs. Each year they attack and kill dozens of people, seizing them in their powerful jaws, then thrashing them to pieces with a violent shaking of the head.

It is not surprising that many people objected when a Brazilian company imported 110 Nile crocodiles in 1989 with plans to breed the animals for their prized skins. Each year, the company hopes to hatch some 3,300 baby crocodiles.

The crocodile farm, located in Osorio, Brazil, has double-walled enclosures and other security features to protect against the escape of the animals. But scientists and other opponents warn that it is just a matter of time before some of the Nile crocodiles escape or are released. The effects on native wildlife could be enormous.

The South American caimans are among the species that would be harmed. These members of the crocodile family range in length from 4 to 11 feet (1 to 3 meters), depending on the species. Scientists doubt that caimans could survive in competition with their larger and much more aggressive relative.

By the 1940s, there were more than 600 million rabbits in Australia. To help reduce the population, a fatal virus disease called myxomatosis was intentionally imported to Australia. Within a few years, the rabbit population was almost completely wiped out.

A small number of rabbits inherited a resistance to myxomatosis, however. They survived and produced offspring that were also resistant. By the early 1990s, the rabbit population had grown to 200 million, and the animals were once again causing extensive damage.

Kudzu

In 1876, as part of the celebrations for the 100th birthday of the United States, a fair, with exhibits from many nations, was held in Philadelphia. Visitors to the fair admired a vine planted as decoration in a Japanese exhibit. Named the kudzu, it had large, grassy green leaves and clusters of reddish-purple flowers. People asked the Japanese for kudzu seeds and seedlings, which they planted in their gardens. In the southern United States, the vine grew year round, unlike in Japan where winter frosts kill the above-ground parts of the plants.

The kudzu was quite common in the South by the early 1900s. But its real dispersal began in the 1930s, when tens of millions of kudzu seedlings were planted, on the advice of soil conservationists, to stop erosion and enrich the soil. By the 1960s, the plants were growing out of control, covering trees and other valued plants.

Getting rid of the kudzu is not easy. Each plant has an enormous root that may weigh as much as 400 pounds (181 kilograms). Growing from that root may be 50 vines, each 100 feet (30 meters) long.

Africanized Bees

In 1956, wild African bees were imported to a laboratory in Brazil. It was hoped that the African bees could be bred with local bees to create a better honey producer. The result of this breeding was a very hardy and aggressive variety of bee.

In 1957, some of the Africanized bees escaped from the laboratory. They attacked and killed local bees, soon earning the nickname killer bees. Brazil's beekeeping and honey industry declined. The decline was temporary, however, as Brazilian beekeepers gradually learned how to manage and breed the Africanized bees. Today, Brazil's beekeeping industry is flourishing. Honey production is significantly greater than before the introduction of the Africanized bee. One major advantage of the Africanized bees is their resistance to a parasitic mite, *Varroa jacobsoni*. This mite kills millions of honeybees in the United States each year.

Since 1957, the Africanized bees have slowly extended their range, moving northward at a rate of 200 to 300 miles (322 to 483 kilometers) a year. In 1984, a swarm was sighted in the United States; other swarms have occasionally been seen since then. The swarms have been trapped and destroyed. It is only a matter of time, however, before Africanized bees spread throughout much of the country.

Superfish

No longer are natural species the only ones being introduced into new habitats. Today, scientists are creating new species in the laboratory. For example, scientists at Auburn University in Alabama have created a new kind of carp. They took growth genes from trout and inserted those genes into the genetic material of carp. The result is a superfish that grows faster and bigger than ordinary carp. Such fish could transform the fish farming industry, enabling fish farmers to produce more food in shorter periods of time.

In 1991, Auburn University scientists planned to release 50,000 young superfish into ponds on the university grounds. Many people are expressing concern that the genetically altered fish could eventually harm native plants and animals. For instance, they are afraid that the fish's fast growth rate might quickly reduce the amount of oxygen in a habitat. This in turn would cause native plants and animals to die from a lack of oxygen.

6

THE EFFECTS OF
HUMAN ACTIVITIES

"A soil that is adorned with tall and graceful trees is not always a favorable one, except, of course, for those trees." The Roman author Pliny the Elder wrote these words in A.D. 77. Now, almost 2,000 years later, people still need to learn this important lesson.

Each year, millions of acres of tropical rain forests are cut down to create farmlands. But the soil that supports a lush rain forest and its many creatures cannot support a field of crops or a range for cattle. In a few years, the land has lost all its fertility. The farmers abandon it, move deeper into the forest and clear another area. The abandoned land erodes and is unsuitable for almost any kind of life.

Human activities have their destructive effects not only in tropical rain forests but everywhere on Earth. Frequently, activities in one region affect people—and wildlife—many thousands of miles away.

Dwindling Wildlife

A major result of the human destruction of natural habitats has been a decline in the populations of many species of plants and animals. Threatened organisms range from cacti of the southwestern United States to pandas of the bamboo forests in China.

Opposite page:
Heavily eroded land lies barren. Erosion and flooding, which often destroy valuable food sources and natural buffers in the environment, can be caused by numerous human activities.

ADAPTING TO PEOPLE

Most wild animals are unable to adjust when people become part of their habitats and make major, rapid changes in the environment. But some organisms have adapted extremely well to the presence of human beings. Cockroaches, silverfish and mice have moved from natural outdoor habitats into people's homes. Mallards are willing to live in small parks. Starlings and herring gulls have expanded their diets to include people's garbage. Woodchucks have benefited from the clearing of forests. Other animals that have adapted to sharing habitats with humans include moles, raccoons, opossums, red foxes, coyotes, white-tailed deer, jays, red-winged blackbirds and gypsy moths.

In North America, for example, populations of many songbirds are declining dramatically. Studies by scientists such as Chandler Robbins, a wildlife biologist at the Patuxent Wildlife Research Center in Maryland, found that between 1978 and 1987 the populations of 20 migrating songbirds that breed in the eastern United States and Canada fell significantly; only 4 species increased in numbers. Northern orioles declined by 26%, yellow-billed cuckoos by 37%, Tennessee warblers by 67% and bay-breasted warblers by 79%.

Several factors are being blamed for the declining songbird populations. One factor is the destruction of tropical forests where many songbirds spend the winter. Another important factor is the fragmentation of the birds' summer habitats: U.S. and Canadian forests are being carved up by suburban sprawl. Still other factors include air pollution, pesticides and an increase in predators such as cats and dogs.

Another group of birds—canvasbacks and other duck species—is being affected by the conversion of wetlands in the midwestern United States to cropland. William K. Reilly, administrator of the U.S. Environmental Protection Agency (EPA) noted in 1991: "In North Dakota, the prairie potholes that remain are crowded with ducks and geese battling for nesting sites, struggling to survive against the onslaught of disease and predators that find easy sport in the cramped breeding grounds. Is it any wonder that duck populations are crashing?"

Pollution also harms wildlife. Chemicals used to kill unwanted weeds, insects and other pests often harm beneficial organisms, too. Sewage dumped into rivers and oceans and fertilizers washed off farmlands change the ecology of aquatic habitats. A 1989 study of fish caught in the Great Lakes found that 90% contained levels of toxic chemicals that were dangerous to wildlife; 25% contained levels dangerous to humans.

Genetic Diversity

Each species has its own unique mix of genetic material. A cow is a cow and not a cauliflower because of the genetic information carried within its cells. But among cows, there also is great variety. Some cows have genes that make them excellent milk producers. Others do not have these genes but may have genes that protect against certain diseases.

As natural habitats are destroyed and populations of a species decline, genetic diversity is diminished. When species become extinct, the information carried in their genes is lost forever. A marked decline in the size of a species' population decreases the genetic diversity of the species and may hasten its extinction. In a large population, there is a

ENVIRONMENTAL BOOMERANGS

Many of people's attempts to "improve" the environment have been short sighted. While solving one problem, they have created new, unexpected problems. Such was the case with DDT (dichloro-diphenyl-trichloro-ethane). In 1939, the Swiss scientist Paul Hermann Müller discovered that DDT was an effective insecticide. The chemical was soon being manufactured in large quantities. It was heavily used in war zones during World War II to kill disease-carrying mosquitoes and other insects. After the war, its use grew and became widespread. DDT spraying programs were very effective in controlling malaria, typhus, river blindness and other human diseases carried by insects. They also were effective in killing insects that damaged crops, thus enabling farmers to produce more food.

Unfortunately, it takes a long time for DDT to break down into harmless substances. When birds such as bald eagles, brown pelicans and peregrine falcons eat insects sprayed with DDT, the DDT accumulates in the birds' bodies and interferes with reproduction. The birds produce eggs with thin shells. Many of the eggs break, resulting in the deaths of the developing chicks.

In the 1950s, populations of bald eagles, brown pelicans and peregrine falcons began to decline in areas where DDT was used. The world paid little attention to the problem, however, until Rachel Carson published *Silent Spring* in 1962. In this widely read book, Carson described the dangers of indiscriminate use of pesticides.

Most uses of DDT were banned in the United States in 1972. Similar action was taken by Canada and several other countries. DDT was replaced by other insecticides designed to kill only specific pests and to break down rather quickly after use. Following the U.S. ban, populations of bald eagles, brown pelicans and peregrine falcons gradually increased—proof that DDT had played a role in their decline.

Root tips hold tlightly to grains of soil and help prevent the soil from washing away. Some plant roots, such as those for alfalfa, can go as deep as 25 feet into the ground.

great deal of genetic diversity. If the population's environment changes, chances are good that some members of the population may be able to adapt to the changes, thus ensuring the population's survival. In a small population, there is much less genetic diversity. The survival of that population is easily threatened by changes in the environment.

Erosion and Flooding

The roots of a single grass plant, if laid end to end, may extend a total of 400 miles (644 kilometers). Imagine the total length of all the roots in a prairie of grass or in a forest of massive trees!

The tips of the roots hold tightly to grains of soil, helping to anchor the plant and preventing running water from washing away the soil. As grasslands are destroyed by overgrazing and poor farming practices and as forests are cut down, erosion increases.

Wind removes some of the soil. In dry areas, spectacular dust storms may occur. In 1934, a dust storm swept thousands of tons of topsoil from the land in Kansas, Oklahoma and Texas. Much of the soil was carried more than a thousand miles eastward before it fell over the northeastern United States and the Atlantic Ocean.

Rainwater and water from melting snow also erode barren land. The water runs quickly off the land, carrying massive amounts of soil with it. Downstream, there may be severe flooding. In Kenya, water measurements were recorded in two adjacent valleys for more than 25 years. When the forest in one of the valleys was cleared for a tea plantation, there was a fourfold increase in water flow following a rainstorm.

Soil carried by streams can cause a form of pollution called siltation. In mountain streams, even small amounts of siltation can prevent the reproduction of aquatic insects that are eaten by trout. Without the insects, trout cannot survive.

Inland wetlands are also critical storage areas for water. During heavy rains, when a river rises and water flows over its banks, surrounding wetlands absorb the runoff. This helps prevent flooding downstream. A study by the U.S. Army

ENDANGERED HABITATS
The Problems

As habitats shrink or are destroyed, animals must compete for fewer vital resources.

THROUGHOUT THE WORLD, living things face extinction because their habitats—the places where they naturally live—re being destroyed. Some threats to habitats are natural, such s storms, volcanic eruptions and lightning-caused fires. Other hreats come from human activities. People cut or burn down orests for timber or to clear the land for farms and other evelopment. They pollute waterways and beaches with oil, esticides, industrial chemicals, sewage and other wastes.

Opposite page: A fire rages out of control in Yellowstone National Park, in Wyoming. *Above:* A dead sea bird is pulled from the oily waters of the Persian Gulf.

An open pit lies at the center of an enormous tract of land that has been destroyed by iron stripmining in the Mesabi Range, Minnesota.

AS PEOPLE CHANGE THE ENVIRONMENT, they may completely destroy a habitat. The many types of plants and animals that lived there become homeless. In other cases, habitats are reduced in size. This reduces the number of plants and animals that can live in the area. For example, when land is strip-mined to recover coal or other mineral deposits, habitats are destroyed. Billions of cubic feet of leftover rocks and soil may be piled to form hills or dumped into wetlands where fish once spawned and ducks nested.

As natural habitats have been destroyed, populations of organisms ranging from the mountain gorilla to various kinds of wild corn have declined. A marked decline in a species' population decreases the species' genetic diversity—that is, the variety of information carried in organisms' genes and passed from one generation to another. As genetic diversity declines, the species loses its ability to adapt to changes in the environment. Its survival is then severely threatened.

Opposite page: An African mountain gorilla rests in the lush vegetation of its habitat. *Above*: Erosion and flooding ruin land and stream habitats by disrupting natural drainage and flow.

Above: A large-mouth bass devours a blacknose dace, completing a step in the never-ending cycle of the food chain.

IN A HABITAT, green plants produce food. Certain animals feed on the plants. Other animals eat the plant-eaters. A change in one part of this food chain can have disastrous consequences for many organisms in the habitat. If, for example, pollutants kill the food producers in a pond, there will be no food for plant-eaters such as water fleas. In turn, fish that feed on water fleas and other plant-eaters will starve.

Corps of Engineers indicated that the loss of wetlands along the Charles River upstream from Boston would cause flood damage averaging $17 million a year.

Coastal wetlands protect against erosion and flooding. They reduce wave action and the speed of incoming waters. In parts of Asia and Latin America, coastal mangrove forests have been cut down and replaced with shrimp ponds. In addition to destroying valued habitats, natural barriers to flooding caused by storms have been eliminated.

"Today, we recognize the terrible toll of generations of uninformed, unthinking and incremental destruction of wetlands."
–William K. Reilly administrator, U.S. EPA

Global Warming

During the next few decades, the Earth's climate is expected to be warmer than at any time in the past 1,000 years. By the middle of the next century, scientists predict that it may be warmer than at any time in the past 125,000 years. The rising temperatures are occurring because of human activities. As fossil fuels are burned—by vehicles, power plants and factories—huge amounts of carbon dioxide are released into the atmosphere. Burning forests to create farmlands and burning wood for fuel also add carbon dioxide to the atmosphere. Rice fields and livestock add large quantities of methane.

At the same time, some of the planet's major storehouses of carbon dioxide are being destroyed. Trees absorb carbon dioxide and use it to produce food. As forests shrink, there are fewer trees to limit the amount of carbon dioxide in the atmosphere.

Carbon dioxide, methane and certain other gases are heat traps. They act like the glass in a greenhouse that allows the sun's energy to enter the greenhouse but prevents heat energy from escaping. Similarly, heat-trapping gases in the atmosphere allow most of the sun's energy to reach the Earth's surface but prevent heat given off by the Earth from escaping into space. As the concentration of heat-trapping gases in the atmosphere increases, more and more heat is trapped and the atmosphere becomes warmer and warmer.

Scientists predict that increases in heat-trapping gases in the atmosphere will cause the average temperature of the Earth to rise by 3° to 8° F (1.7° to 4.4° C) by the year 2050.

Stand a set of dominoes on end and align them in a row, one behind the other. Push the first domino backward. It in turn pushes the domino behind it backward, and a chain reaction occurs. Soon, all the dominoes have been pushed backward and toppled.

When one event initiates a series of similar events, the phenomenon is called the domino effect. In an ecosystem, the domino effect can have serious—and often unexpected—results.

The people of Manaus, a large city in northwestern Brazil, learned this lesson after the surrounding rain forests were cut down. Fish caught in the Amazon River once made up a major part of the people's diet. Some of these fish fed on seeds and fruits that dropped from the forest trees. When the trees were cut down, the fish lost an important food source. As a result, the fish population declined.

At first, the people of Manaus did not understand why there were fewer fish to catch. By the time people understood the relationship between the fish and the trees, all the major forests within 60 miles (97 kilometers) had been destroyed.

A rise of this magnitude will affect every aspect of our environment. Weather patterns will change. Some places will receive more rain than they do today, while other places will become much drier. Oceans will become warmer, which will cause them to expand and flood coastal areas helping to create more violent tropical storms. Land habitats in tropical, temperate and polar areas will become warmer, affecting the organisms that live in those habitats.

As a habitat becomes warmer, many of its plants will no longer be able to live there. If these species of plants are to survive, they will have to migrate toward the poles. Research indicates that many plant species, including many kinds of trees, cannot migrate very fast. They can move perhaps 1.2 miles (2 kilometers) a year. But some scientists predict that ecological zones will shift toward the poles by 60 to 95 miles (97 to 153 kilometers) or more over the next 40 years causing widespread extinction of plants.

A combination of warmer temperatures and less precipitation will result in a decrease in the amount of land suitable for forests. Conversely, there will be an increase in grasslands and deserts. One group of scientists has predicted a 17% increase in the amount of desert land in the world as a result of climate changes expected by 2050. This would significantly decrease the habitats of a broad range of plants and animals.

The flooding of coastal wildlife habitats by rising seas will destroy spawning grounds for many of the world's most important food fishes. Also destroyed will be vital feeding grounds used by migrating birds.

Like plants, animals that cannot adapt to warmer temperatures will have to move if they are to survive. Snails and other slow-moving creatures will not be able to move quickly enough. Animals, such as the caribou herds of the northern tundra, will decline in number as their breeding areas are flooded by rising seas and their food sources are replaced by different kinds of plants.

There is growing evidence that habitats are already being changed by the warmer temperatures of recent years. A study conducted by a team of scientists headed by David W. Schindler, an ecologist at the University of Alberta, noted that the average annual temperature in one part of Ontario rose by about 3.5° F (2° C) between the late 1960s and the mid-1980s. Scientists say that the warmer temperatures have increased the frequency of forest fires and droughts, diminished rainfall and soil moisture and made it more difficult for forests to renew themselves. The warmth also decreased the flow of water into the area's lakes. This has changed the lakes' chemistry, threatening trout and other inhabitants.

Acid Rain

Among the pollutants produced by human activities are sulfur dioxide and nitrogen oxides. Sulfur dioxide is emitted primarily by stationary sources that burn coal as a fuel, including power plants, ore smelters and other industrial facilities. Nitrogen oxides are produced mainly by power plants and motor vehicles. Enormous amounts of these gases are produced: A single industrial smokestack may emit 500 tons of sulfur dioxide daily.

In the atmosphere, sulfur dioxide and nitrogen oxides react with water in the air to form sulfuric acid and nitric acid. Eventually, these acids fall to the ground, usually as part of precipitation. This precipitation is commonly called acid

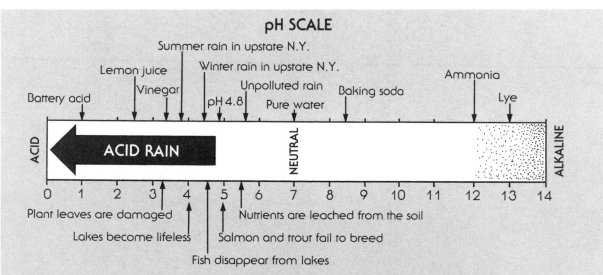

pH SCALE

Summer rain in upstate N.Y.
Lemon juice — Winter rain in upstate N.Y.
Vinegar — Unpolluted rain — Baking soda — Ammonia
Battery acid — pH 4.8 — Pure water — Lye

ACID — ACID RAIN — NEUTRAL — ALKALINE

0 1 2 3 4 5 6 7 8 9 10 11 12 13 14

Plant leaves are damaged
Lakes become lifeless — Nutrients are leached from the soil
Salmon and trout fail to breed
Fish disappear from lakes

Scientists use the pH scale to define levels of acidity. Battery acid is highly acidic; lye is highly alkaline.

The sensitivity of an area's freshwater systems to acid rain depends on the ability of the underlying bedrock to neutralize acid. When most siliceous rock such as granite and quartz are present, the water is highly sensitive to acid. When the rock contains bicarbonate salts that buffer acid, the pH of a lake may remain relatively constant. However, once the lake's buffering capcity is exhausted, a sharp increase in acidity may occur.

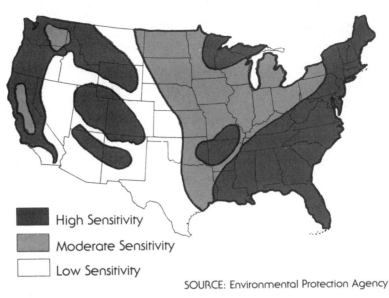

High Sensitivity

Moderate Sensitivity

Low Sensitivity

SOURCE: Environmental Protection Agency

rain. The term *acid deposition* is more accurate, however. Snow, fog and other forms of precipitation can also be acidic. In addition, the acids can be deposited dry, as part of microscopic particles.

Fish and many other aquatic creatures cannot reproduce if the water in which they live becomes too acidic. Trees can be harmed as acids seep into the soil and dissolve soil chemicals needed by the plants. Acids also promote the release of aluminum salts and other toxic metallic substances from the soil. As these metals are carried by rainwater into lakes and streams, they harm aquatic organisms. For instance, aluminum salts kill the eggs of many fish species. They also cause the gills of adult fish to clog with mucus, making them unable to obtain oxygen from the water.

Winds may carry air pollutants far from their source. Acid rain that has destroyed a spruce forest atop Mount Mitchell in North Carolina is believed to have originated in the Ohio and Tennessee river valleys.

Disappearing Ozone

Some 10 to 30 miles (16 to 48 kilometers) above the Earth's surface is a layer of air called the stratosphere. Concentrated in this layer is a form of oxygen called ozone. At ground level, ozone is a pollutant that damages plant leaves and causes other harm to living things. In the stratosphere, though, ozone is a life saver. It absorbs harmful ultraviolet radiation emitted by the sun.

Various pollutants from human activities are destroying the ozone layer. Foremost among these pollutants are chlorofluorocarbons (CFCs). These synthetic chemicals are used as coolants in refrigerators, freezers and air conditioners; as cleaning solvents in the manufacture of electronic circuits; as aerosol spray propellants (a use generally banned in the United States since 1978); and in the manufacture of plastics and foam insulation. Other ozone destroyers include nitric oxide, which is produced by many industries; carbon tetra-chloride, which is widely used as a solvent; and halons, which are used in fire extinguishers.

The greatest destruction of the ozone layer has occurred over Antarctica, but significant declines in ozone concentrations have been measured throughout the world. In 1991, the EPA announced that measurements made from a satellite indicated that about 5% of the ozone layer over the northern United States had been lost since 1978.

Most nations have agreed to stop production of CFCs and certain other ozone destroyers between 2000 and 2010. But because of CFCs already in the hands of users, plus those now entering the marketplace, scientists expect atmospheric concentrations of the destructive chemicals to continue to grow until at least 2005, reaching as much as 30% above the levels in the early 1990s.

As the ozone layer becomes thinner, more ultraviolet radiation is reaching the Earth's surface. Scientists fear that this may greatly harm organisms. There is evidence that an increase in radiation results in a decrease in photosynthesis. Reports indicate that when ozone concentrations over Antarctica decline, so does the amount of photosynthesis in Antarctic waters. The tiny algae in these waters form the basis of all the food chains in the Antarctic ecosystem. Without these algae—and the tiny animals that feed on them—there would be no food for fish, penguins, seals, whales and the other large animals that live there.

7

THREATENED PLANTS AND ANIMALS

In the 1700s and early 1800s, passenger pigeons were the most numerous birds in North America. Some flocks contained a billion or more birds. In 1759, Peter Kalm described "an incredible multitude [flying] so closely together that the sky and the sun were obscured by them." In the 1830s, John James Audubon wrote of a similar migration: "The air was literally filled with pigeons; the light of noonday was obscured as by an eclipse . . . pigeons were still passing in undiminished numbers, and continued to do so for three days in succession."

The vast flocks of birds ate huge amounts of acorns, chestnuts, fruits and insects. They also ate grains and other cultivated crops. People killed the birds because they were pests, because they were good to eat, because they could be fed to pigs or even used as fertilizer. Killing the pigeons for sport was also a popular pastime. Year after year, millions of pigeons were slaughtered until the huge flocks no longer darkened the skies.

By the late 1800s, very few passenger pigeons were left. By 1910, only one was left, a female named Martha. She died in the Cincinnati Zoological Gardens on September 1, 1914. With her death, passenger pigeons became extinct.

Opposite page:
Many human-made accidents can take a devastating toll on the environment. Oil spills, in particular, can destroy or upset major food sources and habitats for hundreds of years. Here, an oil-soaked ocean eagle struggles for survival in Puerto Rico.

71

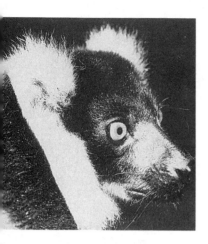

Above and below:
The Madagascar lemur and the dusky sparrow are just two of the many species that are now extinct.

Extinction is Forever

Extinction is not new. It has always happened. But the impact of people's activities has quickened the pace at which plants and animals die out. Today, environmental changes caused by people are the primary causes of extinction.

Of the plants and animals that are native to the United States, 612 were listed by the U.S. Fish and Wildlife Service (FWS) as endangered as of early 1991. Environmentalists believe that many additional species need to be added to the list and given protection. They point out that some species were not listed by the FWS and given protection until it was too late to save them. The Tecopa pupfish, the Santa Barbara song sparrow and Sampson's pearly mussel had to be removed from the FWS list because it became clear that they had become extinct.

Elsewhere in the world, thousands of additional species are threatened. The International Council for Bird Preservation has estimated that more than 1,000 of the 9,000 known species of birds in the world are endangered. Other scientists estimate that at least 25,000 of the world's 250,000 plant species are endangered.

The noted Harvard University biologist E. O. Wilson calculated that as many as 17,500 species may be dying out each year. William Mansfield, deputy director of the United Nations Environment Program, estimated in 1990 that the extinction rate is over 150 species a day, or 54,000 a year. "Biological diversity faces the worst stage of mass extinction in 65 million years," he warned.

Many species are being destroyed before scientists are able to identify and classify them. They are disappearing from Earth without our knowledge of their existence, their beauty, their potential value.

Among the species most threatened by extinction are species with very limited habitats. This problem is especially severe in island habitats in southeastern Asia and Oceania. Numerous species on these islands are endemic—that is, they live nowhere else. Almost half the bird species found in Papua New Guinea are endemic; almost a quarter of the birds of Indonesia are endemic. Some 3,000 species of flowering plants have been identified on New Caledonia, an island in the southwest Pacific; 80% of them grow nowhere else.

Violets and Other Plants

African violets are among the most popular houseplants. They are raised on windowsills and tabletops in homes all over the world. In Africa, however, the wild relatives of these plants are not doing as well. Wild African violets are among the most endangered plants on Earth. Their main habitat is the forests of the Usambara Mountains of Tanzania. The main threat to their survival is deforestation. People are rapidly cutting down the forests, using the timber for building material and as fuel for cooking fires.

Some two dozen cacti species that grow in the southwestern United States are known to be endangered. Among them is a small hedgehog cactus, commonly called the black lace cactus, known to exist in a single locality in Texas. There are two main threats to its survival. One is development of the land; the other is collection by commercial collectors and by people who want to have the cacti in their own homes or gardens.

Also endangered is the Knowlton cactus. It is no larger than a 25-cent coin, though its pink flowers are twice that size. This cactus is found only in northern New Mexico and nearby parts of Colorado. The main threat to its survival occurred when most of its habitat was flooded by the San Juan Dam. Commercial collection of the Knowlton cactus has been another serious problem.

Another plant that is threatened by overcollecting in the wild is ginseng. The roots of this small herb are highly valued, particularly in China. Many people believe the ground, dried roots cure a broad range of medical problems, including cancer, diabetes and headaches, and help slow the aging process. In South Korea, a large ginseng root is said to add 10 years to a person's life. For more than 200 years, people in North America have gathered ginseng for export to China. The species has become extinct in some parts of Canada and the United States as a result. Today, ginseng is cultivated but collecting plants from the wild continues.

FACING NEW DANGERS

Kirtland's warbler is a small songbird with a very restricted habitat. It nests only among jack pines growing on sandy soil that is unique to a small area in Michigan. Furthermore, it builds nests only among grasses growing beneath trees that are between 8 and 22 years old.

Most of the warbler's nesting grounds are part of Huron National Forest. To prevent the jack pines from growing too large, foresters periodically harvest some of the older trees. They also burn sections of the forests, to allow the growth of new jack pines. Together with other protective measures, these steps have enabled the warbler to survive.

But what will happen to Kirtland's warbler if global warming raises temperatures in Michigan? Jack pines will not grow in a warmer climate. Other trees, such as white pines and red maples, will invade the forest. If temperatures rise high enough, even those trees may not survive; instead, Huron National Forest could become a grassland.

Elephants and Other Animals

In 1979 there were 1.3 million African elephants. Within only 10 years, the population fell more than 50% to only 625,000. The major cause of this decline has been illegal shooting of the animals for their tusks to meet a worldwide demand for ivory. In 1989, in an effort to slow the rapid decline in the number of elephants, Britain banned all imports of ivory. Soon thereafter, many other nations also agreed to ban ivory trade.

The giant panda of central China is endangered largely because it has lost most of its habitat and food supply to development. Pandas live in damp bamboo forests, where they feed almost exclusively on bamboo leaves and shoots. The forests slowly disappeared as much of the land has been cleared for agriculture.

Cricket frogs were once common on Canada's Pelee Island in Lake Erie. By 1990 they were almost gone. Ecologists believe a primary cause for the frogs' disappearance is the heavy use of fertilizers and pesticides on island farms. The chemicals wash off the farmland into drainage ditches where most of the frogs lived.

Only a few hundred Mediterranean monk seals remain, the remnants of a once-abundant colony. A main cause for their demise has been the enormous amounts of sewage and other wastes dumped into the Mediterranean Sea by ships, factories and communities.

Achatinella, an entire genus of Hawaiian tree snails, are endangered. Some of the species have already become extinct. The populations of several additional species are so small that they too will soon disappear. One threat to their existence is a predator snail, *Euglandina rosea*. The predator was introduced into Hawaii to control the African snail, but the African snail is comparatively large, so *Euglandina* didn't attack it. Instead, it has preyed upon the native tree snails.

People Are Hurt, Too

Natural habitats are places where people can relax and enjoy activities such as hiking and swimming. Our lives are immea-

DAMMING SHIVA'S RIVER

The Narmada River in central India flows westward for about 800 miles (1,287 kilometers) before emptying into the Gulf of Cambay. It is among India's most sacred rivers, for it is believed to have sprung from the body of Lord Shiva, one of the three great Hindu gods.

In the state of Gujarat a huge dam is currently being built that will greatly change the appearance of part of the Narmada. When the Sardar Sarovar dam is completed, it will create a reservoir covering almost 150 square miles (388 square kilo-meters)—more than six times the area of New York City's Manhattan.

Despite its immense size, Sardar Sarovar is only a small part of a much larger plan to dam the Narmada River. When the proposed project is completed sometime in the 21st century, it will consist of 30 major dams, 150 medium-sized dams and 3,000 smaller dams. Supporters of the project say it will produce large amounts of electricity, provide irrigation waters to help feed millions of people and protect people living downriver from the devastating effects of flooding. Critics consider the project an environmental catastrophe. They say the dams will submerge large areas of fertile agricultural lands and scarce forests, ruin soils and introduce health problems.

The project will also displace an estimated 1.5 million people, including tribal people who had previously been forced out of forests by logging operations. Where will the people go? How will they cope in new areas far from their homelands? What help will they receive?

surably enriched by natural forests, seashores and marshes and by the sight of warblers, dolphins and antelope.

As natural habitats disappear and wild plants and animals dwindle in number and in diversity, humans also suffer. Sometimes, the effects on people are deadly. The destruction of forests in Asia's Himalaya Mountains has caused massive erosion and flooding. Thousands of people living downstream from the mountains have been killed by such floods.

Threats to Indigenous Tribes

Natural habitats are home to hundreds of indigenous tribes who have been natives of their environment for hundreds of years. They know how to live in the habitats and how to use the resources without destroying them or the environment. They also have valuable knowledge about the plants and animals in their habitats—knowledge that could benefit people elsewhere.

Today, most indigenous people live in tropical forests. As outsiders have come into the forests, the natives have suffered greatly. Such has recently been the fate of the Yanomami

FIGHTING OVER RESOURCES

In 1969, a brief war broke out between El Salvador and neighboring Honduras. A primary cause of the war centered on the large influx of Salvadorans into Honduras: The Salvadorans were fleeing their overcrowded country in search of jobs or lands. This led to increasing friction between the Salvadorans and the Honduran farmers.

In 1983, thousands of people were killed in northeastern India during widespread ethnic violence. Native Assamese demanded the deportation of Bengalis who had fled there from their native Bangladesh in search of food and other basic necessities.

Fighting over limited resources is expected to grow in the coming years as increasing population plus rising consumption increases demands on natural resources.

Indians, who live in the Amazon rain forest of Brazil. During the late 1980s, after government studies indicated the presence of gold in the region, a gold rush began. More than 45,000 miners arrived in the forests where the Yanomamis live. They cut down trees to create landing strips for their planes. They dumped mercury into the waters. They introduced tuberculosis, the common cold and other diseases to which the Yanomamis have no natural immunity. By late 1990 Brazil's Indian Missionary Council estimated that 1,500 of the 9,000 Yanomamis had died as a result of the gold rush. International pressure helped force the Brazilian government to take steps to save the Yanomamis and their habitats. The government began to evacuate miners and to prohibit non-Indians from entering the mineral-producing lands where the Yanomamis live.

Food Supplies

People obtain many valuable products from plants and animals. As the human population grows, there is an increasing need for these products. Yet declining habitats threaten supplies of everything from food to fuel.

More than 80% of the world's food supply comes from only 20 plant species. Three of these species—corn, wheat and rice—provide 65% of the food supply. Scientists continually try to improve crops. They try to change the genetic makeup of the plants so they yield more food, are more resistant to pests, can grow in drier environments and so on. The main source of genetic material for these breeding efforts are wild or locally cultivated relatives of the crops. For example, wild relatives of domesticated corn and tomatoes still live in South American forests. Wild coffee trees grow in West African forests and wild sugarcane is found in forests of the South Pacific. If these plants disappear, genes that could expand world food production also disappear.

Many foods of potentially great economic value are known only to small local populations: quinoa, a grain eaten in Bolivia; fonio, a cereal important in Gambia and Guinea; karite, a nut, widely eaten in Ghana and Nigeria.

A SECOND CHANCE

Sometimes, we are given a second chance to save a species. In the 1950s, the government in India's Manipur State declared that the brow-antlered deer was extinct. The species had been a victim of hunting and loss of habitat. But the government statement was premature: A few of the deer still lived in the area's humid, grassy wetlands. In the 1970s, legislation to protect wildlife was introduced in Manipur State. In 1975, an aerial survey found 15 brow-antlered deer in the high grasses.

By 1990, the number had risen to almost 80. The brow-antlered deer is still among the world's most endangered mammals. But its gradual comeback has encouraged conservationists to hope that the threat of its extinction may be receding.

Another species once believed extinct is the ivory-billed woodpecker. This exceptionally handsome bird once flourished in the southern United States and in Cuba, stripping bark from dead or dying older trees to feed on beetles. The last definite

sighting of an ivory-bill in the United States was in 1941. The last proven sighting in Cuba was in the 1970s—until 1986, when several ivory-bills were seen in a forest in eastern Cuba. Following the latest sighting, the Cuban government banned all logging in the ivory-bill area and took other protective measures. Because ivory-bills are very shy, it is probably impossible to determine how many still live. But now that their habitat is protected, their chance of survival is improved.

Of indirect importance to our food supplies are animals that pollinate crops, disperse seeds or control weeds and destructive insects. For example, banana, avocado, breadfruit, mango, date, cashew, carob and clove plants depend on bats for their survival in the wild.

Pollution also affects our food supplies. Global warming will mean a loss of land on which to raise crops. One area that is expected to be severely affected is the southwestern United States. A study found that a 3° F (1.7° C) warming combined with a 10% drop in precipitation would decrease viable land in arid regions of the west by nearly one-third. Farming in the southeast would also be harmed. The EPA has warned that soybean and corn yields in the southeast could fall by more than 90% in coming years.

Medicines

Up to 50% of the medicines in use today contain ingredients that originally came from living organisms. Penicillin, a widely used antibiotic, is derived from a common mold. Digitalis, used to treat heart disease, was originally extracted from a common wildflower called foxglove. Vincristine and

ENDANGERED

As of May 1991, the U.S. Fish and Wildlife Service had listed a total of 612 native plant and animal species as endangered or threatened: 457 endangered and 155 threatened. (NOTE: One genus of Hawaiian snails is counted as a single species because scientists are uncertain about the actual number of species.) Here are a few examples of more commonly known animals.

Akepa, Hawaii (honeycreeper)
Ala Balik (trout)
Albatross, short-tailed
Alligator, American
Antelope, giant sable
Armadillo, giant
Baboon, gelada
Bat, gray
Bear, brown or grizzly
Beaver
Beetle, American burying
Bison, wood
Blackbird, yellow-shouldered
Blindcat, Mexican (catfish)
Boa, Mona
Bobcat
Bushwren, New Zealand
Butterfly, Schaus swallowtail
Camel, Bactrian
Cat, Andean
Cat, leopard
Cat, tiger
Catfish, Yaqui
Cavefish, Ozark
Cheetah
Chimpanzee
Chinchilla
Condor, Andean
Cougar, eastern
Crane, black-necked
Crayfish, Nashville
Crocodile, American
Crow, Hawaiian
Darter, amber
Deer, key
Deer, musk
Dog, African wild
Dolphin, Chinese river
Dove, cloven-feathered
Duck, white-winged wood
Dugong
Eagle, bald
Egret, Chinese
Elephant, African & Asian
Falcon, American peregrine
Ferret, black-footed
Finch, Laysan (honeycreeper)
Flycatcher, Seychelles paradise
Fox, Northern swift
Frog, Israel painted
Frog, Panamanian golden
Gazelle, Arabian
Gecko, Monito

Gibbons
Goat, wild
Goose, Aleutian Canada
Gorilla
Grackle, slender-billed
Grebe, Atitlan
Gull, Audouin's
Hare, hispid
Hartebeest, Swayne's
Hawk, Hawaiian
Hermit, hook-billed
Hog, pygmy
Hornbill, helmeted
Horse, Przewalski's
Hyena, Barbary
Ibex, Pyrenean
Ibis, Japanese crested
Iguana, Fiji crested
Impala, black-faced
Jaguar
Jay, Florida scrub
Kakapo
Kangaroo, eastern gray
Killfish, Pahrump
Kingfisher, Guam Micronesian
Langur, capped
Lemurs
Leopard
Lion, Asiatic
Lizard, blunt-nosed leopard
Lynx, Spanish
Macaw, indigo
Mallard, Mariana
Manatee, West African
Marmoset, buff-headed
Marsupial-mouse, large desert
Minnow, loach
Monkey, black colobus
Monkey, spider
Moth, Kern primrose sphinx
Mouse, Key Largo cotton
Mussel, dwarf wedge
Ocelot
Ostrich, Arabian
Otter, Camaroon clawless
Owl, Anjouan scops
Panda, giant
Panther, Florida
Parakeet, golden-shouldered
Parrot, Australian
Pearly mussel, Alabama lamp
Pelican, brown
Penguin, Galapagos

Pheasant, Mikado
Pigeon, Azores wood
Pigeon, Puerto Rican plain
Plover, piping
Porcupine, thin-spined
Possum, Leadbeater's
Prairie chicken, Attwarer's grearer
Prairie dog, Utah
Puma, Costa Rican
Pupfish, Ash Meadows Amargosa
Quail, Merriam's Montezuma
Quetzal, resplendent
Rat, Fresno kangaroo
Rhinoceros, black
Robin, scarlet-breasted (flycatcher)
Salamander, desert slender
Salmon, chinook
Sculpin, pygmy
Sea lion, Stellar
Seal, Caribbean monk
Shiner, Cape Fear
Shrike, San Clemente loggerhead
Shrimp, California freshwater
Sloth, Brazilian three-toed
Snail, Virginia fringed mountain
Snake, Concho water
Snake, San Francisco garter
Sparrow, Cape Sable seaside
Sparrow, dusky seaside
Spider, Tooth Cave
Spinymussel, Tar River
Squirrel, Carolina northern flying
Starling, Ponape mountain
Stork, wood
Tern, California least
Thrush, large Kauai
Tiger, Tasmanian
Toad, African viviparous
Tortoise, desert
Turtle, Alabama red-bellied
Vicuna
Wallaby, banded hare
Warbler (wood), Bachman's
Whale, blue
Whale, finback
Whale, humpback
Whale, sperm
Wolf, gray
Wombat, hairy-nosed
Woodpecker, ivory-billed
Woodrat, Key Largo
Yak, wild
Zebra, Grevy's

vinblastine, used to treat certain types of cancer, are derived from the rosy periwinkle. Cortisone, used to treat rheumatoid arthritis, was originally derived from wild yams. Quinine, once the only drug available to fight malaria, is obtained from the bark of cinchona trees.

People's knowledge of the medicinal value of plants is very limited. Only a very tiny percentage of plants have been analyzed for their chemical properties. The extinction of unknown plants means that some potentially life-saving medicines may never be found.

When a promising medicine is found, however, conflicts between two worthy goals may result. One of the most exciting medical stories in recent years has been the development of the drug taxol. Samuel Broder, director of the U.S. National Cancer Institute calls taxol "the most important new drug we had had in cancer in 15 years." Studies indicate that taxol damages cancer cells without harming normal cells. The drug has helped people who have not been helped by other drugs. Taxol is extracted from the bark of the Pacific yew tree. It takes the bark of 2,000 to 4,000 trees to produce 2.2 pounds (1 kilogram) of taxol. Treating one patient requires the bark of six 100-year-old trees. These trees are scattered through the old-growth forests of the Pacific Northwest, habitats of the northern spotted owl. Thus the desire to clear-cut the forests to obtain taxol conflicts with the desire to save the forests for the owl and other wildlife. The hoped-for solution is synthesizing taxol, so that large quantities can be manufactured in laboratories. This procedure has been successful with other chemicals.

Wood and Wood Products

In Asia, Africa and South America, people use much of the wood they cut for fuel. As forests have shrunk, the task of gathering enough wood to meet basic heating and cooking needs becomes harder and harder. In some parts of India, a person must spend two days gathering a week's worth of wood for his or her family. When firewood is unavailable, the families burn dried cow dung; this creates health problems. It also prevents the dung from being used to fertilize farmlands, which in turn means poorer crop yields.

In North America, Europe and Australia, most of the wood is used for construction or manufactured products. Vast amounts of wood is cut into lumber, which is used for buildings, furniture, boats, barrels and thousands of other uses. Papermaking is another major wood-based industry. Paper is used to make newspapers and books, writing and copying papers, corrugated cardboard, toilet tissue, food cartons and even money. Wood-based chemicals include cellulose compounds that are used to make plastic films and rayon fibers, as well as cellulose nitrate, which is a raw material used in the manufacture of gunpowder and other explosives. Forests are being cut faster than they are being replaced, threatening the Earth with severe shortages of wood and wood products in the future.

Other Products

As natural habitats are destroyed, people will also face shortages of other valued resources. Some of these resources are known to us and are currently being exploited. Additional materials of potential value, however, are continually being found and studied. Scientists recently discovered a chemical produced in the salivary glands of octopuses that may become a valuable pesticide. Guayule, a shrub native to deserts in Texas and Mexico, produces rubber and may be an important future source of this widely used material.

Threats to Human Health

In Kenya, mosquitoes that infect people with malaria are native to the hot lowlands. In recent years, however, the mosquitoes have expanded their range to the surrounding highlands. "There are strong indications that their presence is one of the results of the greenhouse effect," said environmentalist Herik Othieno of Kenya.

As warming temperatures change habitats, pests such as malarial mosquitoes are expected to adapt more easily than most other organisms. The warmer weather is expected to expand their ranges. For example, bat-borne rabies may increase as the vampire bats of South and Central America extend their range northward.

The pollution of habitats by sewage and industrial wastes kills organisms valued as food sources. Pollution from pulp mills in western Canada forced the closing of shellfish beds along the coasts of Vancouver Island. Dumping of a suspected cancer-causing chemical by a factory on the Housatonic River in Massachusetts led to a ban on fishing downstream in Connecticut.

Taking Responsibility

The destruction of natural habitats does much more than flood homes, limit supplies of natural resources, threaten health and limit recreational possibilities. It also raises a moral issue. As James Baker, a biologist with the U.S. Fish and Wildlife Service, said: "We don't have the moral right to let one species die. Ethics is not only a question of man's behavior to man, but also includes taking responsibility for our environment." Living species need to be saved not for our sake but for their sake.

8

SAVING PLANTS AND ANIMALS

 Huge herds of buffalo once roamed the grasslands of North America. In 1851, a man who had long lived on the plains wrote a vivid description of these herds: ". . . from bluff to bluff on the north and on the south and up the valley to the westward—as far as the eye could reach—the broad valley was literally blackened by a compact mass of buffalo, and not only this—the massive bluffs on both sides were covered by thousands and thousands that were still pouring down into the already crowded valley, and as far as the eye could reach, the living dark masses covered the ground completely as a carpet covers the floor."

It is estimated that there were some 60 million buffalo before European settlers moved into the American west. As people converted the grasslands into farmland and as railroads expanded into the area, the number of buffalo killed each year grew until the slaughter reached gigantic proportions. The buffalo were killed for food and for their hides. Some were killed for political reasons: Politicians thought that by killing the buffalo they could also destroy the Indians who depended on the animals. Hundreds of thousands of buffalo were killed for the "sport" and "fun" of killing large animals.

The last large herd of buffalo was killed in 1883. Only small groups of the animals remained, mostly in hard-to-reach

Opposite page:
Because humans pose the greatest threat to the Earth's habitats, the most effective method of stemming destruction is to change harmful human activities. Protests, boycotts and other political involvement are a few ways to help change the world.

places. A census conducted in 1899 counted only 541 buffalo. Fortunately, laws were passed to protect these survivors and several preserves were set aside for them. The species has slowly made a comeback. Today, the population has reached an estimated 75,000. None of these animals roam across open grasslands, however. All live in preserves or as managed herds on ranches.

Scientists and environmentalists agree that the most effective and least expensive means of preserving wildlife is by preserving wild habitats. There are, however, a number of additional steps that can—and in some cases, must—be taken if threatened species are going to have a reasonable hope of surviving.

Breeding Programs

Deforestation in Suriname has destroyed much of the native habitat of blue poison dart frogs. A few of these endangered animals have found a new home in the rain forest exhibit at the National Aquarium in Baltimore, Maryland. Scientists spent five years recreating the frogs' natural environment. Final proof of their success came when the little frogs reproduced.

Programs to breed captive endangered animals are under way at zoos all over the world. The underlying objective of these programs is to keep the species in existence while efforts are made to restore native habitats.

One of the most highly publicized efforts to save a species through a captive breeding program involves the California condor, the largest land bird in North America. At the beginning of 1988, only 27 California condors were known to exist; all were in captivity. Several months later, the first chick conceived in captivity hatched. By the beginning of 1991, the condor population had risen to 40.

Test-Tube Babies
On April 27, 1990, the Henry Doorly Zoo in Omaha, Nebraska, became the proud parent of Mary Alice. The baby was a rare Bengal tiger. What made her even more special was

that she was the first tiger conceived by *in vitro* fertilization. In other words, she was a test-tube cub.

In vitro is Latin for in glass. *In vitro* fertilization involves obtaining eggs from a female and sperm from a male. The eggs and sperm are mixed together in a glass laboratory dish. The fertilized eggs are cultured until cell division occurs and embryos begin to develop. Then, one or more embryos are implanted in the mother-to-be. This might be the female that donated the eggs, or it might be another female—a surrogate mother. In Mary Alice's case, it was the latter. Her surrogate mother wasn't a Bengal tiger, but a Siberian tiger.

The success of the Bengal tiger experiment holds great promise for helping endangered species survive. *In vitro* fertilization and embryo implantment make it possible for scientists to mate animals that live in different places—for instance, a male in a North American zoo and a female in a European zoo. It may also be possible to freeze fertilized embryos from zoo animals and implant them in wild animals. This would help increase the genetic diversity among small, isolated populations of a species.

Foster Parents

Each pair of whooping cranes usually lays two eggs. However, when the eggs hatch, the parents rear only one chick. The second chick is ignored and almost always dies. In 1966, biologists decided to remove one of the two eggs from some whooping crane nests. The eggs were put in the nests of sandhill cranes. The foster parents incubated the eggs and raised the young birds as if the youngsters were their own.

Since those initial experiments, other species have also been helped by foster programs, including peregrine falcons and New Zealand shore plovers. Foster parents need not be of a different species. Ospreys that live in some places are so heavily contaminated with pesticides that they lay eggs that do not hatch. These eggs can be replaced with eggs taken from ospreys that live in less contaminated places. This practice helps maintain osprey populations in polluted habitats until the habitats have been cleaned up.

BIG BAD WOLVES?

As people have moved into new areas, one of their first acts often has been to eliminate predators that might interfere with raising domesticated animals. Governments had traditionally encouraged the killing. For example, between 1883 and 1918, government-supported programs killed more than 80,000 wolves in Montana.

Now, governments are changing their attitudes. Environmentalists and wildlife managers are convincing people not only that there are moral reasons for saving these species but also that the predators are an essential part of natural habitats. Wolves can help control populations of elk and deer that otherwise become so large that they destroy their own habitats.

Not everyone is convinced that reintroducing predators is a sensible idea. Plans to reintroduce gray wolves to Yellowstone National Park in Montana were strongly opposed by neighboring sheep and cattle ranchers. They feared that roaming wolves would kill large numbers of their animals.

A study conducted in Minnesota where there are wolves—and many more livestock animals than around Yellowstone National Park—indicates that the ranchers' fears are excessive. Between October 1989 and October 1990, wolves in Minnesota killed a reported 959 farm animals. Almost all the prey were turkeys; only 36 were cattle and 103 were sheep.

Reintroducing Species to the Wild

Hundreds of attempts have been made to introduce zoo-bred animals into their native habitats. Some of the attempts have been successful. Others, though they failed, provided biologists with valuable information that will improve the success of future efforts.

Often, reintroductions fail for the same reasons that originally endangered the species. For example, one of the reasons a lizardlike reptile called the tuatara disappeared from the New Zealand mainland was the introduction into its habitat of predators such as the Polynesian rat. If tuataras are to be successfully reintroduced, the threat of predators must first be eradicated.

Between 1984 and early 1991, 89 rare monkeys called golden lion tamarins, which had been raised in captivity as part of the Golden Lion Tamarin Conservation Program, were reintroduced to Brazil's Atlantic rain forest—the only place in the world where the species naturally lives. Thirty-five of the tamarins survived, and by early 1991 they had given birth to 51 youngsters.

In the Alps, the bearded vulture, or lammergeier, is being re-established, after having been extinct there for many decades. A related species, the Negev lappet-faced vulture, is native to the Negev desert in southern Israel. In 1988, only one pair of birds remained in the wild in Israel. That year, Tel Aviv University's research zoo succeeded in breeding Negev vultures in captivity for the first time, raising hopes of saving the species.

Among the most successful animals to be reintroduced has been the peregrine falcon, which almost became extinct in the 1970s because chemical pesticides interfered with its reproduction. Now, thanks to large-scale, captive-breeding programs, the species is making an encouraging comeback. The birds have been released not only into their traditional habitats but also into cities. Tall city structures with ledges resemble the cliffs on which peregrines naturally nest; and a city's large populations of pigeons, sparrows and starlings provide a plentiful supply of food. People out for early-morning walks are becoming accustomed to seeing peregrines diving at speeds of up to 150 miles (241 kilometers) per hour. The birds grab their prey in midair, then carry it back to a high ledge to enjoy a leisurely breakfast. In 1988, a peregrine living in a tall building in Boston hatched two chicks—the first wild chicks born in Massachusetts in 40 years. In 1990, 13 chicks were born in New York City, where peregrines nest atop office buildings, churches, bridges and even a hospital.

Seed Banks

One way to help save the genetic diversity of plants is to save their seeds. Seeds do not take up much space. They do not require the expensive maintenance needed by animals or growing plants. Around the world, botanical gardens, agricultural research stations, universities and other organizations have established seed banks. In the Philippines, there is a bank for seeds of different rice varieties. In India, there is a chick-pea bank. Canada has a collection of barley seeds. Ethiopia has a collection of legume seeds.

When seeds of a particular species are gathered for a bank, they must first be cleaned. Next, they are dried in a desiccator to remove any water. The seeds are then placed in vials and frozen. At intervals of about five years, some of the seeds are thawed out and their germination rates are tested.

The seeds of some species cannot be dried or frozen. In such cases, a garden of 50 plants is established. These 50 plants must reproduce so that the garden is self-perpetuating. In an ordinary backyard or on a typical household windowsill, it isn't a crisis when a plant dies. In a garden where the 50 plants of a species may be irreplaceable, however, there isn't much margin for error.

Protective Laws

Many animals do not stay in one place. Squirrels run from one person's property to a neighbor's tree. Bears wander through forests from one state to the next. Birds migrate between continents. Fish and whales travel great distances in the oceans.

People don't stay in one place either. People from one state go deer hunting in another state. Gardeners travel to wild habitats to unearth cacti or wildflowers to take home to their backyards. Tourists from one nation visit another nation, where they are offered souvenirs made from bird feathers, animal shells or rare woods.

People who stay home can harm wildlife, too. They order bulbs of endangered plants from catalogs. They acquire rare animals as pets. They buy furniture made from rain forest trees. They kill beneficial animals under the mistaken belief that the animals are pests.

Wildlife protection requires laws that limit the harm caused by people. Local laws can be helpful, but national and international laws are essential. Governments must do more than just pass laws, however. They must enforce those laws. Often laws have not been successful in protecting wildlife because insufficient efforts were made to implement the laws.

When legislation is strong and widely supported, it can be a powerful tool for conserving wildlife, as the following example demonstrates.

CITES

The Convention on International Trade in Endangered Species of Wild Fauna and Flora (CITES) is an international treaty that took effect in 1975. It has been signed by more than 100 countries.

CITES offers two different levels of protection to endangered plants and animals. Species listed in Appendix I of the treaty cannot be traded between countries except in a few exceptional circumstances. Species in Appendix II can be traded between countries but controls are placed on such trade. For example, trade of species listed in Appendix II is controlled through permits and is allowed only when considered nondetrimental to the survival of wild populations. Each nation that signs CITES is responsible for enforcing regulations on imports of protected organisms and products into their country or territories.

One group of animals that is being helped as a result of CITES are the flying foxes. These bats are found throughout tropical areas in Africa, southeast Asia and the Pacific

POACHED PARROTS

Most pet parrots in the United States have been bred in captivity. But each year, an estimated 250,000 parrots are imported into the country. Large numbers of parrots are also imported into Japan and several European countries.

Most of the imports are from wild populations. Many are imported legally. Others are captured by poachers, who then trade the birds illegally. They smuggle the parrots out of one country and into another. The U.S. Fish and Wildlife Service estimates that about 50,000 parrots are smuggled into the United States each year just from Mexico.

The number of wild parrots that reach people's homes is only a small part of the story. Up to 90% of illegally caught birds are believed to die before they reach their destination. Baby birds are killed as they are snatched from their nests. Birds in transit suffocate to death, die of hunger or thirst or are killed by overdoses of tranquilizers.

Throughout their tropical habitats, parrot populations are declining. At least 30 species of parrots are endangered, including the imperial parrot, the palm cockatoo and the scarlet macaw. Also endangered is the hyacinth macaw—the largest and most spectacular of the world's 340 species of parrots.

Some people do not care if parrots are endangered. Many may even encourage the scarcity of a species. They will pay huge sums of money to own a rare bird. A hyacinth macaw may sell for $10,000 or more. As long as smugglers can find a market for exotic parrots, they will continue to capture wild birds. If nobody wanted the birds, nobody would try to catch and sell them.

Islands. They are extremely important animals, for they play critical roles in the life cycles of many plants. While working on her Ph.D. degree at Boston University, Marty Fujita studied the economic value of flying foxes. She documented more than 300 plant species that depend on flying foxes for pollination or seed dispersal. "At least 134 of these plants yield products that are used by humans," noted Fujita. "More than 450 products, including medicinals, food, drinks, fruits, dyes, tannins, timber, fiber and fuelwood, are derived from these plants."

Flying fox populations have declined and disappeared in many places. Rain forest destruction is a major cause. Another major cause is human consumption. People in some places consider bats a delicacy. Among these places is Guam, one of the Marianas Islands in the western Pacific and a territory of the United States. The little Marianas fruit bat is extinct and another species is endangered because of overhunting. As local bat populations declined, the people of Guam imported more and more bats for consumption. According to Gary J. Wiles, a wildlife biologist with the Guam Division of Aquatic and Wildlife Resources, an estimated 230,000 bats were imported to Guam between 1975 and early 1990. This seriously threatened bat populations throughout the Pacific.

In 1987, nine species of flying bats were placed on CITES' Appendix II. However, the U.S. Fish and Wildlife Service (FWS) did not enforce the restrictions. Two years later, due to the efforts of conservation groups such as Bat Conservation International, seven species of flying bats were given Appendix I status. In the spring of 1990, FWS sent two wildlife inspectors to Guam to enforce the trade ban. Almost immediately, the number of imported bats took a nosedive—and flying foxes disappeared from the freezers at local supermarkets.

Community and Backyard Ecology

In Maryland, volunteers build platforms in the Patuxent River. In New York state, people raise platforms on Long

Island marshlands. Their objective is to lure ospreys. The birds once were common along the east coast of the United States. Then their numbers decreased because of pesticides and because the trees in which they nested were cut down. Pesticide levels have declined, but the fallen trees have not been replaced. The platforms are proving to be an attractive alternative. In 1976, Long Island had 69 active osprey nests. By 1991, there were more than 200.

In Texas and Oklahoma, volunteers plant native trees and wildflowers along highways. This helps preserve the species of plants as well as the birds, insects and other animals that feed on them. In addition, the natural beauty of the plants provides pleasure to passing motorists—and saves communities millions of dollars in grass cutting and other maintenance costs.

In Connecticut, the Department of Environmental Protection gives out free plans for bat houses to encourage people to build homes for the flying mammals. Six of the seven types of bats that live in Connecticut are insect eaters; the other species eats insects and preys on other bats. Helping the bat population helps people, too. One little brown bat—Connecticut's most common bat—can eat 600 mosquitoes in a single hour!

These are just three examples of the ways in which individuals can help provide habitats for wildlife. Each effort is valuable. Each makes a difference, not only to the future of Earth's plants and animals, but also to the future of people.

"What is a man without the beasts? If all the beasts are gone, men would die from a great loneliness of the spirit. For whatever happens to the beasts soon happens to man."
     –Chief Seattle, 1854

9

HABITATS FOR THE FUTURE

Ecologists have discovered that in any one community of organisms, some species may be more important than others. These species have been called keystone species. If a keystone species disappears from a community, the entire ecology of that community is severely disturbed. There is likely to be a rapid decline and perhaps even a complete collapse of the community.

In the Chihuahuan Desert of Arizona, the kangaroo rat is a keystone species. This rodent—which has long hind legs and hops like a kangaroo—is well adapted to the desert environment. It can survive without drinking water; it obtains sufficient water from the digestion of the seeds that compose its diet. Biologists James H. Brown and Edward J. Heske from the University of New Mexico fenced in 24 plots in the Chichuahuan Desert. The plots were in an area near a transitional zone between the desert and a grassland ecosystem. Each plot was about half the size of a football field. Some plots contained kangaroo rats, others did not. Over a period of 10 years, there were no significant changes in the plots with kangaroo rats, but the plots without rats took on many characteristics of a grassland. Grasses began to grow. Plants with large seeds replaced those with small seeds. Plant litter accumulated on the ground. Snow melted more slowly. Populations of other rodents grew but the number of seed-eating birds declined.

Opposite page:
A flock of penguins frolics on the ice in Antarctica. The vast frozen lands of the North and South poles still remain the largest untouched habitats on Earth.

Brown and Heske believe that two behaviors of the kangaroo rats are responsible for maintaining desertlike conditions. First, the rats prefer large seeds to small seeds; thus plants that produce large seeds have a poor chance of surviving. Second, the rats disturb the soil as they search for food, bury the food and create burrows; this appears to aid decomposition of litter and to make it easier for birds to find seeds to eat.

Scientists have identified only a few keystone species. In the sandhills of the southeastern United States, gopher tortoises appear to be a keystone species. In the kelp forests off the coast of California, sea otters are a keystone species. In tropical rain forests, certain wasps are keystone species. Some 900 species of figs can be pollinated only by wasps—and each species of fig has its own particular species of wasp to pollinate it. The figs, in turn, are a basic food source for numerous insects, fish, birds, mammals and other animals.

In some communities, keystone species are seemingly insignificant creatures like wasps and kangaroo rats. Elsewhere, the keystone species may be large predators or grazers. On Panama's Barro Colorado Island, the ocelot, mountain lion and jaguarundi are believed to have been the keystone species. These wild cats preyed on smaller predators, including raccoons and coatimundis, and they helped limit their populations. These wild cats of Barro Colorado Island have been exterminated. In their absence, populations of smaller predators, which feed on birds and bird eggs, have boomed. Several species of birds have become extinct on the island as a result.

Many scientists believe that the keystone concept demonstrates the importance of preserving entire habitats. Only by saving habitats, with their complex diversity of species, can we ensure that all those species have a chance to survive. And only by preserving precious habitats can we hope to ensure that one extinction does not lead to a whole series of extinctions.

Expanding Protected Lands

Protection may come in many forms, large and small. In 1990, the Central American nation of Belize expanded its Cockscomb Wildlife Sanctuary to nearly 100,000 acres (40,470 hectares). The expansion provided important protection for the jaguar, a sleek cat whose population has been greatly reduced as a result of hunting and habitat destruction.

The Nature Conservancy, a private conservation organization, bought the Gray Ranch in New Mexico. The ranch covers 321,703 acres (130,193 hectares) astride the Animas Mountains. Habitats include desert, grassland, chaparral and coniferous forests. Among the great diversity of life on the ranch are at least 718 species of plants, including 71 that are considered rare or endangered. There are an estimated 75 species and subspecies of mammals, including about 20 species of bats. Approximately 150 species of birds breed on the ranch. *The Albuquerque Tribune* called the purchase "profoundly generous and far-sighted." It commented: "The Conservancy's quietly and patiently conducted move is much better proof of concern for the state's future than the reams of waffle-talk issued by supposedly pro-economic-development folks . . . ."

In Connecticut, landowners on Lord Cove, a tidal marsh on the Connecticut River, have donated 208 acres (84 hectares) of valuable habitat to The Nature Conservancy. Together with land protected by the state and by a local land trust, this brings a total of 600 acres (243 hectares) at Lord Cove under permanent protection. The habitat is popular with many types of birds, including bald eagles.

In many places, natural habitats have been fragmented by development. There is no way for wildlife to move from one suitable habitat to another, except through housing tracts and other developments. Many animals will not do this; others die in the attempt. One solution is to construct pathways between the habitats. Often called greenways, these may link forests, meadows, riversides, even urban parks. In Wisconsin, the Elroy-Sparta State Park Trail crosses 32 miles (51 kilometers) of dairy country. In Virginia, the Washington and Old Dominion Railroad Regional Park Trail runs along a former railroad bed. In California, two greenways totaling 800 miles (1,287 kilometers) are being built around San Francisco Bay. People use such trails for hiking, bicycling and other pastimes. All sorts of animals use them, too—a use that will be increasingly critical as global warming makes some habitats unsuitable for the animals.

Countries can work together to expand protected habitats. In 1922, Italy established Gran Paradiso National Park in the Italian Alps. Later, France established Vanoise National Park on its side of the border. In 1972, the two countries agreed to expand the parks' common boundary to more than 8 miles (13 kilometers). Ibexes, chamois and other animals are able to move back and forth between the two parks in search of food, mates and so on.

For whooping cranes, humpback whales and other migratory species, it is not sufficient to protect only one habitat. Both feeding grounds and breeding grounds must be protected. The routes traveled by the migrating animals and essential resting places along those routes must also be protected.

Paying for Protection

Protecting habitats can be costly. There are maintenance costs plus the costs of guarding the habitats against improper use. If the desirable land is not yet protected, there is the cost of buying it. Such costs are particularly burdensome for poorer countries. By 1988, developing countries had debts to international banks and other creditors that totaled more than $900 billion. Simply paying interest on these loans consumed a large portion of the countries' earnings.

Conservationists in rich countries in North America and western Europe are playing critical roles in preserving their own countries' environments. In addition, these conservationists are helping poorer countries save valuable habitats.

One technique that has been successful is called the debt-for-nature swap. A conservation group buys some of a country's

ENDANGERED HABITATS
The Solutions

Clean and undisturbed habitats enable species to thrive.

PROTECTING HABITATS may come in many forms. Instead of dumping sewage and other wastewaters directly into a river or ocean, they can first be treated to remove nutrients, toxic metals and other harmful chemicals. Instead of filling in wetlands or using them as dump sites, they can be protected for the use of migrating birds and other wildlife. Beaches and other wildlife habitats can be closed to people during animals' nesting seasons.

Opposite page: Solid waste is treated and then discharged at a plant in Metropolis, Illinois. *Above:* A Laughing Gull is perched atop a sign at the Cedar Island National Wildlife Refuge in North Carolina.

EVERYONE CAN PLAY VALUABLE ROLES in protecting habitats and saving endangered species. People can be active in campaigns to save old-growth forests and other unique habitats. They can protest harmful practices, such as the use of fishing methods that kill dolphins, turtles and birds. They can boycott products made from endangered species or from materials that require destruction of important habitats. They can limit use of natural resources by recycling. And they can support elected officials who work to protect the environment.

Star Kist

DOLPHIN SAFE

PRISONER OF VANITY

Fur coats, once symbols of glamour, are now recognized as the end... of misery, suffering, and death for millions of animals.

DON'T BUY FUR!

Join the Campaign For a Fur-Free America

TRANS-SPECIES UNLIMITED

National
(717) 322-3252

New York City
(212) 966-8490

Chicago
(312) 227-8...

Opposite page: Members of Kids Against Pollution rally for their cause in New York City. *Above:* Many companies now use special emblems to inform consumers about environmentally safe practices. *Left:* A protester displays a placard at an anti-fur rally.

PEOPLE CAN PROMOTE BIOLOGICAL DIVERSITY around their homes and in their community by planting a variety of trees, shrubs and wildflowers. The focus should be on species that are native to the area. Hedges and fields of wild grasses provide shelter and protection for rabbits and other small animals. Fruit-bearing trees and shrubs attract birds. The scents and colors of flowers attract butterflies and other insects. Birdfeeders, bat houses and water basins also help attract wildlife.

Opposite page: Red azaleas, mountain pinks and basket-of-golds create the basis for a beautiful rock garden and useful human-made habitat. *Right:* Tiny pine siskins take advantage of a well-stocked birdfeeder.

Above: A lioness suckles her young cubs during a peaceful moment in Kenya.

IF THE EARTH IS TO CONTINUE to be home for tigers and other wildlife, we must protect their habitats. Tracts of land must be set aside as parks and refuges. Money must be appropriated to guard and maintain protected lands. In addition, there is a need to restore habitats that have been turned to other uses or that have been damaged by various activities. Deforested hills can be planted with trees, polluted rivers can be cleaned, filled wetlands can be redug and eroded beaches can be rebuilt.

debt from its international creditors at discounted prices—often because the creditors no longer have much hope of ever collecting the debt. The group then forgives the debt in return for certain environmental commitments from the country.

The first debt-for-nature swap occurred in 1987. Conservation International paid $100,000 for a $650,000 debt that Bolivia owed to a bank. Conservation International then agreed to forgive the $650,000 debt if Bolivia would protect and manage a 3.7-million-acre (1.5-million-hectare) area around the Beni Biosphere Reserve.

In 1990, the U.S. government indicated that it might follow the lead of private conservation groups and allow some of the money owed to the United States to be used instead for conservation projects. A major supporter of the plan was William K. Reilly, administrator of the U.S. EPA, who said: "The aim of debt-for-nature swaps is straightforward: to increase the resources allocated to the environment while reducing burdensome debt. It is visionary. It is practical. And it works."

Restoring Habitats

In addition to conserving natural habitats, there is a need to restore habitats that have been used for other purposes or that have been damaged by various activities. Deforested hills can be planted with trees, rivers filled with litter can be cleaned, sand-dune vegetation killed by beachgoers can be replaced.

Some 10,000 years ago, melting glaciers created numerous wetlands in the American Midwest. Now called potholes, these wetlands became important habitats for migratory birds. As people settled the Midwest, they began to drain the potholes and turn the land into farms. Populations of ducks were particularly hard hit. One way to help the birds is to restore some of the lost habitats. In Minnesota, the U.S. government leased land from farmers and turned it back into potholes. At first, ducks only stopped briefly, en route to other places. As the marsh vegetation grew thicker, however, the birds remained to breed.

RECYCLED TREES

Each year, Americans buy some 35 million natural Christmas trees. When the holiday season has ended, there are 35 million dead trees to be discarded. Many end up in landfills, taking up increasingly scarce space. One alternative is to grind up the trees. The chips can then be mixed with yard wastes to produce a nutritious mulch for gardens and parks.

In Louisiana, old Christmas trees are being put to another use: to rebuild wetland habitats that are being destroyed by waves and rising tides. One successful technique uses a double row of fences made of netting strung between posts. The fences are built in shallow areas near the shore. The old Christmas trees are compressed and dumped between the two fences. When the tide flows out of the marsh, sediment carried by the water is trapped by the trees. Before long, a natural dam has formed that prevents the marsh from being lost to the tides.

One restoration project began with the collection of trees in 1987. By 1990 marsh grass was being planted on new land that had formed. The grass should help trap even more sediment.

A century ago, more than a million roseate spoonbills, storks and other wading birds lived in the Florida Everglades. Today, there are fewer than 5,000 wading birds. Less than 50 Florida panthers remain. Bass and catfish are contaminated with mercury. Sawgrass has been replaced by cattails, which remove oxygen from the wetlands and suffocate the organisms at the bottom of the Everglades food chain. Massive development in southern Florida has created most of these problems, but there are hopes that at least some of the problems can be solved.

The Everglades' main source of water is Lake Okeechobee. The lake has become polluted with runoff from farms carried into the lake by the Kissimee River. Between 1961 and 1971, the U.S. Army Corps of Engineers had turned the meandering river into a straight canal. In the process, 45,000 acres (18,211 hectares) of wetlands were lost—wetlands that had been home to birds and, equally important, had removed pollutants from the water. Now the Army Corps of Engineers is restoring the Kissimee River to its natural state.

Conserving Resources, Limiting Pollution

In May 1989 a forest grew in Kansas City's Volker Park. It consisted of 1,800 stacks of newspapers, each 5 feet (1.5 meters) tall. Each stack of newspapers represented a pine tree 40 feet (12 meters) high. This phantom forest represented the amount of wood cut for one printing of Kansas City's Sunday newspaper.

The display illustrated how much habitat must be destroyed for only one edition of one city's Sunday newspaper. Cities all over world printed newspapers on that Sunday, as well as on the remaining 364 days of that year.

Recycling paper is one of many valuable ways to conserve resources and reduce habitat destruction. A ton of paper made wholly from wastepaper saves 17 trees. It also saves enough energy to power an average home for six months, plus thousands of gallons of water and some 3 cubic yards (2.3 cubic meters) of landfill space.

Improved farming methods help prevent soil erosion, thus conserving farmland and protecting nearby aquatic habitats from the destructive effects of siltation. For example, in contour plowing, the land is plowed parallel to the contours of sloping land. Each furrow acts like a miniature terrace. It slows water, giving the water time to soak into the soil. On broad prairies, farmers can plant rows of trees between fields. Such clusters of trees are called windbreaks—they break the force of winds, thereby limiting wind-erosion. The rows of trees also provide homes for wildlife.

The pollution caused by chemical pesticides can be avoided by using biological methods of pest control. One such method is to fight pests with their natural enemies. In China, insects that attack sugarcane are controlled with parasitic wasps—at one-third the cost of chemical pesticides. Another type of biological control is natural pesticides. These are being made using everything from crab shells to grasshoppers. The crab-shell pesticide is made by grinding up the shells, which contain a substance called chitin. When spread onto fields, fungi in the soil convert the chitin to substances that kill pests that feed on crop roots.

Laws that require industries to limit pollution can be extremely helpful, particularly if they are written without loopholes and if they are strictly enforced. A great deal of damaging pollution has been avoided through the use of devices that trap pollutants before they enter the environment. Catalytic converters in automobiles and electrostatic precipitators in factory smokestacks are examples. Unfortunately, many gains made in the effort to limit pollution are quickly wiped out—by the rise in the number of automobiles on the road, the increased consumption of paper products and other demands of the world's growing population.

Slowing Population Growth

If natural habitats and wildlife are to be saved, human population growth must be slowed. Some progress has been made in recent years. In 1990, the birth rate in developing nations averaged 3.9 children per woman. This was a major improvement since 1960, when the rate was 6.0. A birth rate of 3.9, however, is still considered to be too high because it is significantly higher than the death rate. In industrialized nations, the birth rate averages 1.9 children per woman; this is slightly below the death rate. However, the populations of industrialized nations, such as the United States, continue to grow because of immigration and because the higher birth rates of the recent past mean there are more women of child-bearing age.

Population growth has a momentum similar to that of a moving car. If the car is speeding down a highway and the driver removes his or her foot from the gas pedal, the car will continue to move forward. Only gradually will it slow to an eventual stop. Even if the birth rate is stablized at acceptable levels, the world's human population will continue to grow.

At what point will the human population stabilize? Projections made in the late 1980s suggested that the population might level off at 10.2 billion people by the year 2085. Only a few years after this projection, population experts at the United Nations indicated that it may have been too optimistic. "Some analysts now believe that 10 billion will be reached by 2050, and growth will probably go on for another century after that, unless some substantial further progress can be made in reducing fertility," noted a 1991 United Nations Population Fund report, which suggested that population may eventually level off at about 11.6 billion—more than twice as many people as currently live on Earth. This sobering outlook does not bode well for the planet's other species.

Roles for Everyone

Throughout the world, scientists are studying ways to protect habitats and save endangered species. They are learning about the intricate relationships within natural communities. They are studying life cycles, food chains and reproductive behavior to better understand the needs of individual organisms. They are trying to solve specific problems, such as

MISSION TO PLANET EARTH

On October 4, 1957, the Soviet Union launched a 184-pound (83-kilograms) ball named *Sputnik 1* into orbit around the Earth. It was the start of a new age: the space age. Since that historic day, several thousand spacecraft have been sent aloft. They have carried out a wide variety of missions, adding greatly to our knowledge and understanding of the universe.

Many space missions have focused not on distant stars but on the Earth itself. Landsat satellites have mapped surface features. The *Earth Resources Technology Satellite* has surveyed natural resources. The Seasat satellite used radar to take 350,000 wind measurements over the world's oceans.

Data gathered by such satellites have enabled scientists to monitor urban development, measure changes in ozone concentrations over the South Pole, learn the rate of forest clearing in the Amazon, locate underground oil reserves, forecast crop harvests, track the path of air pollution, map strip-mining damage and discover spiral eddies in the oceans.

While such achievements have been tremendously valuable, many scientists believe that a more unified approach to data measurements is needed. Instead of gathering wind data from one satellite passing over one part of the ocean and ocean current data from a second satellite passing over another part of the ocean, both tasks should be performed simultaneously by instruments aboard the same satellite. This will enable the scientists to better understand how the Earth works as a system. It will help them to better predict changes in the Earth's environment.

This thinking forms the basis behind Mission to Planet Earth. This international program will use both space and ground-based measurement systems. Central to the program will be the Earth Observing System (EOS), a 15-year mission scheduled to begin in 1998. The U.S. National Aeronautics and Space Administration (NASA) plans to launch six EOS satellites. Present plans call for two series of polar-orbiting satellites, EOS-A and EOS-B. There will be three identical satellites in each series, launched consecutively, each with a 5-year lifetime.

Each satellite will weigh 7,700 pounds (3,493 kilograms) and will be packed with instruments that gather data at the same time from the same point. This will allow data to be compared and shared between experiments without being subject to errors that are introduced when information is gathered in different places at different times.

Questions that scientists hope to answer as a result of Mission to Planet Earth include: How is the atmosphere changing? How much carbon dioxide is being taken up by the oceans? What governs rainfall patterns? How do clouds influence global temperatures?

As Mission to Planet Earth gets under way, it is appropriate to recall the words of Wernher von Braun, the German-born engineer who played a central role in the development of manned space flight: "The more we go into space the more we'll find that the most interesting planet to study from space is Earth."

"We shall not cease from explo-
ration,
And the end of all our exploring
Will be to arrive where we
started,
And know the place for the first
time."

–T. S. Eliot

how to remove oil from birds caught in oil spills and how to limit harmful pollutants from power plants.

The knowledge gained by scientists is being put to use in numerous ways: to rebuild swamps, to save the whooping crane, to limit the need for chemical pesticides, to create bacteria that turn hazardous wastes into harmless substances, to maintain genetic diversity, to use natural resources more wisely.

It is everyone's responsibility to support such efforts and ensure that they continue. Every one of us can contribute; every one of us can make a difference.

There are many ways in which you can help protect habitats and save the wildlife with which we share planet Earth. Here are just 10 suggestions:

• Work on local campaigns to clean up beaches, marshes and other habitats.

• Promote biological diversity on your property and in your community by planting trees, shrubs and wildflowers; use species that are native to your region.

• Reduce or eliminate the use of hazardous pesticides and household chemicals; use alternate, less harmful products instead.

• Boycott products made from endangered species or from materials that require destruction of important habitats.

• Limit your use of natural resources by recycling and by buying products made from recycled materials.

• Dispose of harmful chemicals such as used motor oil and antifreeze by taking them to a center with a recycling program.

• Conserve fossil fuels (and limit the pollution they cause) by buying energy-efficient appliances, limiting use of air conditioners, and walking or biking instead of using a car.

• Write to elected officials and urge them to support legislation to slow deforestation, protect wildlife and preserve valuable habitats.

• Join and support organizations that work on environmental issues

BE ACTIVE IN BAT CONSERVATION— BUILD A BAT HOUSE

Begin with a board called a "one-by-eight" that is eight feet long. The best wood is rough cedar, but pine will do if you rough up the inside surfaces so bats will be able to hold on.

1. Study the plan, the size of each piece and how the pieces go together.

2. Mark and cut the board.

3. Nail together the sides, front, back, and interior divider.

4. Nail on the roof so that it is even with the back. Roof will overlap on sides and front.

5. Tack the floor with a nail through each side. Leave heads sticking out slightly. This enables you to pull nails out to open and clean box later on.

6. Add hinges to the floor.

7. Screw a 2-inch corner bracket on the roof for mounting the house.

8. Mount the house on a tree 12 to 15 feet above the ground. Nail through corner bracket at top and through landing platform at bottom.

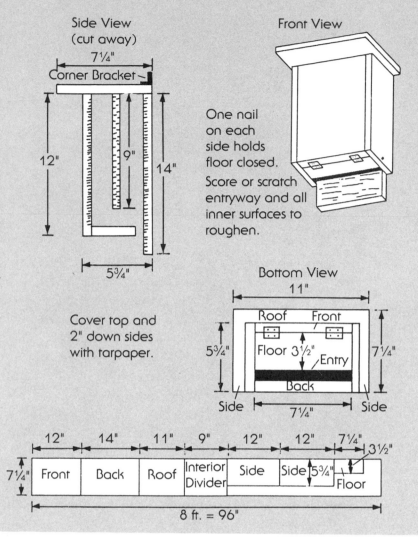

Side View (cut away)

Front View

One nail on each side holds floor closed.

Score or scratch entryway and all inner surfaces to roughen.

Cover top and 2" down sides with tarpaper.

Bottom View

• Educate other people by sharing information on environmental issues: lend books and articles, write letters to newspapers, ask to talk on local radio programs, help organize school and community workshops.

Now Is the Time to Act

In the coming years, will you—and your children and your children's children—be able to visit a tall grass prairie? Will there be whales to watch off the coast of California? Will there be pandas in the forests of China and koalas in the forests of Australia?

Will there be room for rhinos?

GLOSSARY

acid rain Rain and other precipitation that is polluted by acids, particularly sulfuric acid and nitric acid.

air pollution The presence in air of acids, smoke and other materials that damage the air's quality.

biological magnification The concentration of certain substances in organisms along a food chain. This is an important mechanism in concentrating pesticides and heavy metals in organisms such as birds and fish.

bryologist A scientist who studies mosses.

carnivores Animals that eat other animals.

clear-cutting A forest management practice that involves cutting all the trees within an area at one time.

climate The average weather condition in a region over a long period of time.

climatologist A scientist who studies climates and how they change.

conservation Measures taken to protect and improve forests and other natural resources.

consumer An animal that eats a producer, the product of a producer or another animal.

decomposers Organisms such as bacteria that break down organic matter into simpler substances.

deforestation The destruction of a forest.

desertification The spread of desertlike conditions in arid and semi-arid regions.

ecology The study of how living things relate to one another and to their environment.

ecosystem All the organisms in an area and their interactions with one another and with their nonliving surroundings.

endangered species Species of plants and animals that are in danger of becoming extinct.

erosion The wearing away of soil, rock and beaches by wind or water.

estivation A period of time in the summer when some animals become inactive to conserve water and energy.

ethologist A scientist who studies animal behavior.

extinct No longer in existence. The term is used in relation to species or populations of organisms rather than to a single organism.

fertilizer A chemical added to the soil to improve plant growth.

food chain A series of organisms in an ecosystem. Each organism feeds on the previous organism in the chain; the initial organism in the chain is a green plant.

food web The complex relationship formed by interconnecting and overlapping food chains.

fossil fuels Oil, coal and natural gas, formed from the remains of organisms that lived millions of years ago.

genetic diversity Variations within the genetic material of a species. The greater the amount of variation, or diversity, the better the species' chances of survival.

global warming A rise in atmospheric temperatures caused by increased concentrations of heat-trapping gases such as carbon dioxide and methane.

habitat The place or region where an organism naturally lives.

heavy metals Metallic elements such as mercury, lead and arsenic. Even at low concentrations, these elements can harm organisms, and they tend to accumulate in food chains.

herbivores Animals that eat only plants.

hibernation A period of time in the winter when some animals become inactive to conserve heat.

niche The part an organism plays in an ecological community.

nucleic acid A type of molecule including deoxyribonucleic acid (DNA) and ribonucleic acid (RNA). These molecules store genetic information and control cellular activity and the making of proteins.

omnivores Animals that eat both plants and animals.

ornithologist A scientist who studies birds.

ozone A form of oxygen. A molecule of ordinary oxygen consists of two atoms of oxygen;

a molecule of ozone consists of three atoms of oxygen.

ozone layer The concentration of ozone in the stratosphere that protects the Earth from ultraviolet radiation.

pesticide A substance used to kill mosquitoes, weeds and other pests.

photosynthesis The process by which an organism uses sunlight to make its own food.

plankton Organisms that float or drift on or near the surface of a body of water.

producer An organism, such as green plant, that makes food through the process of photosynthesis.

reclamation The restoration of a habitat to its former condition after it was polluted or destroyed.

recycling The process of using something over and over again or of converting discarded materials into new products.

silt Very fine particles of soil, sand or rock carried by moving water.

threatened species A species that is likely to become endangered in the forseeable future.

ultraviolet radiation An invisible form of short-wave radiation emitted by the sun.

water pollution The presence in water of materials that damage the water's quality.

watershed The area of land that contributes water to a river.

wetlands Swamps, marshes, estuaries and other areas that are regularly saturated by water and whose vegetation is adapted for life in saturated soil conditions.

FURTHER READING

Anzovin, Steven (ed.). *Preserving the World Ecology*. New York: H. W. Wilson, 1990.

Berger, John J. *Restoring the Earth: How Americans Are Working to Renew Our Damaged Environment*. New York: Alfred A. Knopf, 1985.

Brown, Lester R., et al. *State of the World 1991*. Washington, DC: Worldwatch Institute, 1991.

Diamant, Rolf, et al. *A Citizen's Guide to River Conservation*. Washington, DC: The Conservation Foundation, 1984.

DiSilvestro, Roger L. *Fight for Survival*. New York: John Wiley & Sons, 1990.

Dwyer, Augusta. *Into the Amazon: The Struggle for the Rain Forest*. San Francisco: Sierra Club Books, 1991.

Earthworks Group. *50 Simple Things You Can Do to Save the Earth*. Berkeley:Earthworks Press, 1990.

Lamb, Marjorie. *2 Minutes a Day for a Greener Planet*. San Francisco: Harper & Row, 1990.

McNeely, Jeffrey A., et al. *Conserving the World's Biological Diversity*. Washington, DC: World Resources Institute, 1990.

Merilees, Bill. *Attracting Backyard Wildlife*. Stillwater, MN: Voyageur Press, 1989.

Newman, Arnold. *Tropical Rainforest*. New York: Facts On File, 1991.

Owens, Mark, and Delia Owens. *Cry of the Kalahari: Seven Years in Africa's Last Great Wilderness.* Boston: Houghton Mifflin, 1985.

Schreiber, Rudolf L., et al. *Save the Birds.* Boston: Houghton Mifflin, 1989.

Steger, Will, and Jon Bowermaster. *Saving the Earth: A Citizen's Guide to Environmental Action.* New York: Alfred A. Knopf, 1990.

Teal, John, and Mildred Teal. *Life and Death of the Salt Marsh.* New York: Ballantine Books, 1969.

Thorne-Miller, Boyce, and John Catena. *The Living Ocean: Understanding and Protecting Marine Biodiversity.* Washington, DC: Island Press, 1991.

In addition, the following periodicals regularly cover issues concerning habitat and species loss:

Audubon. National Audubon Society, 950 Third Avenue, New York, NY 10022

Environment. Heldref Publications, 1730 M. L. King Jr. Way, Berkeley, CA 94709

Environmental Action. Environmental Action, Inc., 1525 New Hampshire Avenue NW, Washington, DC 20036

Greenpeace. Greenpeace USA, 1436 U Street NW, Washington, DC 20009

National Geographic. National Geographic Society, P.O. Box 2895, Washington, DC 20013

National Wildlife and International Wildlife. National Wildlife Federation, 8925 Leesburg Pike, Vienna, VA 22184

Natural History. American Museum of Natural History, Central Park West at 79th Street, New York, NY 10024

Science News. Science Service, Inc., 1719 N Street NW, Washington, DC 20036

Sierra. Sierra Club, 730 Polk Street, San Francisco, CA 94109

World Watch. Worldwatch Institute, 1776 Massachusetts Avenue NW, Washington, DC 20036

Directories of government agencies and private organizations concerned with environmental issues:

Conservation Directory. National Wildlife Federation, 8925 Leesburg Pike, Vienna, VA 22184.

Directory of Environmental Organizations. Educational Communications, Box 35473, Los Angeles, CA 90035.

Directory of National Environmental Organizations. U.S. Environmental Directories, Box 65156, St. Paul, MN 55165.

INDEX

A

Acid rain, 67–68
Adaptations, 20–23
Africa, 58–59, 73
Alaska, 53
Alfalfa, 20, 30, 64
Algae, 12, 13, 43, 44, 46
Alpine forest, 36
Amphibians, 33
Anemones, 45
Anhingas, 15, 18
Animals
    decline of, 61–64, 66
    endangered, 71–81
    growth and development of,
      11–12
    introducing, 56–59
    people and, 62
    population of, 17
    saving, 83–91
Audubon, John James, 71
Australia, 57–58

B

Bacteria, 11, 14
Baker, James, 81
Barnacles, 45
Bats, 21, 90, 91
Bays, 42
Bears, 14
Bees, 58–59
Beetles, 13, 14
Behavioral adaptations, 20–21
Benthos, 46

Bioluminescence, 45
Birds
    bills of, 18, 30
    decline of, 62–63, 66
    endangered, 72
    land habitats and, 30, 33, 34
    saving, 85, 86–87, 89
    water habitats and, 46
Birth rate, 55, 99–100
Bittern, 20–21
Blackflies, 34
Braun, Wernher von, 101
Brazil, 57, 59, 66
Breeding programs, 84–85
Brown, James H., 93, 94
Bryologists, 7
Buffalo, 83–84
Butterflies, 22

C

Cacti, 7, 20, 73
Camels, 33
Canopy, 27
Carbohydrates, 13
Carbon dioxide, 42, 65
Caribou, 34
Carnivores, 13, 44
Carson, Rachel, 63
Cascade Range, 37
Cats, 15
Cells, 11, 43
Central Park, 17, 20
Chaparral, 31–32
Chlorofluorocarbons (CFC s), 69

Cities, 35
CITES treaty, 89
Clear-cutting, 51, 52
Climatologists, 7
Closed habitats, 41
Clover, 15
Coast Range, 37
Communities, 17–18
Community ecology, 7, 90–91
Condor, 37, 84
Conifers, 29, 36
Conservation hints, 102–103
Conservation International, 97
Conservationists, 95, 96–97
Consumers, 13–14
Contour plowing, 99
Coral reefs, 9, 43
Cortisone, 79
Coyote, 14
Crabs, 12, 47
Cranes, 85, 96
Crocodiles, 57
Crossbills, 18, 20
Currents, 44

D

Dams, 50, 75
DDT, 63
Death rate, 55
Debt-for-nature, 96–97
Deciduous forests, 28, 36
Decomposers, 14
Deer, 77
Deforestation, 9, 51, 73, 84

109

Photo Credits

Page 4, © Peter Menzel/Stock, Boston, Inc.; p. 10, © Len Rue, Jr./Stock, Boston, Inc.; p. 24, © Owen Franken/Stock, Boston, Inc.; p. 33, © Ellan Young/Photo Researchers, Inc.; p. 35, © Peter Menzel/Stock, Boston, Inc.; p. 38, © Jerry Howard/Stock, Boston, Inc.; p. 48, © Jack Spratt/The Image Works; p. 52, © Stephen Ferry/Gamma-Liaison; p. 60, © William B. Jones/USDA Soil Conservation Service; p. 63, © G. Ronald Austing/Photo Researchers, Inc.; p. 70, © Clemens Kalischer; p. 72 (top), © Tom McHugh/Photo Researchers, Inc.; p. 72 (bottom), © Bill Wilson/Photo Researchers, Inc.; p. 82, © Mike Mazzaschi/Stock, Boston, Inc.; p. 92, © Michael C. T. Smith/Photo Researchers, Inc.; p. 101, NASA.

Cover, portfolio opener/Problems, © M. Bruce/The Picture Cube; portfolio page 2, © Morrison/The Picture Cube; portfolio page 3, © P. F. Bentley/Photoreporters; portfolio pages 4–5, © Grant Heilman/Grant Heilman Photography; portfolio page 6, © Yann Arthus-Bertrand/Peter Arnold, Inc; portfolio page 7, © USDA Soil Conservation Service; portfolio page 8, © Runk/Shoenberger/Grant Heilman Photography.
Portfolio Solutions: Opener, © Grant Heilman/Grant Heilman Photography; portfolio page 2, © Will McIntyre/photo Researchers, Inc.; portfolio page 3, © Runk/Schoenberger/Grant Heilman Photography; portfolio page 4, © Joel Gordon; portfolio page 5, © Joel Gordon; portfolio page 5 (top), courtesy of StarKist; portfolio page 6, © Grant Heilman/Grant Heilman Photography; portfolio page 7, © Lefever/Grushow/Grant Heilman Photography; portfolio page 8, © G. Ziesler/Peter Arnold, Inc.

Art on pages 8, 16, 21, 26, 45, 64: Sonja Kalter.

Photo Research by Inge King.